# Usborne
# Making Sweets

Abigail Wheatley & James Maclaine

Designed by Helen Edmonds & Anna Gould

Illustrated by Sarah Walsh
Photography by Howard Allman

Recipe consultant: Catherine Atkinson
Food preparation by Maud Eden

# sweet skills

The tips on these pages will help you with specific techniques featured in some of the recipes in this book.

## melting chocolate

1 For best results, find a heatproof bowl that fits snugly into a saucepan, so the bottom of the bowl doesn't touch the bottom of the pan – there should be a gap of around 2cm (1in) between them.

2 Fill the saucepan a quarter full with water. Put it over a medium heat. When the water bubbles, take it off the heat.

3 Break up the chocolate and put it in the bowl. Wearing oven gloves, lower the bowl into the pan. Leave for 5 minutes, then stir until the chocolate melts.

## Drizzling melted chocolate

Scoop up some melted chocolate on a teaspoon. Hold the spoon over a sweet. Tip the spoon, then move it over the sweet in a zigzag shape, leaving a trail of chocolate.

## filling a piping bag

1 Push a piping nozzle down to the pointed end of a piping bag. If you're using a plastic piping bag, snip the end off first.

2 Stand the bag point-down in a mug or glass. Open up the bag and turn the top edge over the rim of the mug or glass.

3 Spoon in some filling. Stop when the bag is half full. Unfold the top edge. Make a twist in the bag, just above the filling.

## shaping balls

You can shape sweet mixture into a ball by rolling it between the palms of your hands, like this.

## shaping eggs

To make an egg shape, first roll a ball (see above). Then, pinch and roll part of the ball into a point. Pat the other end to flatten it slightly.

## shaping sausages

To roll a sausage shape, put a ball of sweet mixture on a flat surface and roll it back and forth, like this.

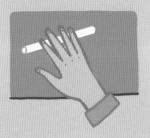

## Rolling out

1 Dust a clean surface and a rolling pin with a little icing sugar. Put the sweet mixture on the surface.

2 Roll over the sweet mixture with the rolling pin going from front to back, then from side to side until the mixture is the thickness you need.

If it gets sticky, sprinkle on a little more icing sugar.

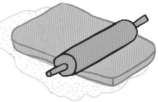

3 If you want to straighten the edges, take a clean ruler, dust it in icing sugar and gently press against the edges of the mixture.

## cutting out

1 Put a cutter over your rolled-out sweet mixture and press down gently, but don't twist.

2 Lift up the cutter. If the sweet comes too, hold the cutter over a tray and gently push the sweet, so it falls out.

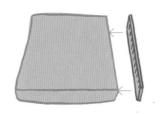

3 If the sweet stays behind, use a small spatula or a blunt knife to lift it up and put it on the tray.

# sweets & treats

lime & coconut snowballs

coconut ice

# jelly sweets

 ## Ingredients:

6 gelatine leaves
135g (4½ oz) packet of jelly
75ml (3 fl oz) boiling water

You will also need a heatproof bowl, a large shallow pan, a jug and around 4 silicone ice cube trays.

## Makes around 40

These sweets are made using bought jelly, gelatine and silicone ice cube trays. Use any shape of tray and any flavour of jelly you like.

1 Put the leaves of gelatine in a mug with some cold water for 5 minutes. Then, remove the jelly from its packaging and cut it into tiny pieces.

2 Pour some boiling water into the heatproof bowl, to warm it. After a minute, tip the water away.

3 Pour the 75ml (3 fl oz) boiling water into the warmed bowl. Add the jelly and leave for two minutes. Stir until the jelly has dissolved completely.

4 Take the gelatine out of the mug with your fingers and add it to the warm liquid jelly. Whisk with a fork to mix, then leave for a few minutes.

5 Fill the shallow pan half full with water. Put it over a medium heat. When the water bubbles, turn down the heat as low as you can.

Keep in an airtight container for up to 5 days.

10

# powdered gelatine

If you can't find gelatine leaves, you can make these sweets using a 12g (¼oz) sachet of powdered gelatine. Skip step 1 and sprinkle the powder over the warm liquid jelly at step 4 instead.

This sweet was made using strawberry jelly.

Lime jelly

Pineapple jelly

These jelly sweets were made in an ice cube tray with round, wavy-edged holes.

Orange jelly

Wear oven gloves.

6 Lower the bowl into the pan. Leave for 2 minutes. Then, turn off the heat. Stir until the gelatine has dissolved completely. Carefully remove the bowl from the pan and leave it to cool for a few minutes.

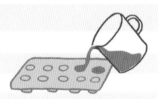

7 Put the jelly mixture into the jug. Then, pour it into the holes of the ice cube trays. Carefully move the trays to the fridge. Leave for 30 minutes or until the jelly sets.

8 Take the trays out of the fridge. Remove the jelly sweets by pushing each one out from the bottom of its tray.

# toffee crunch

 Ingredients:

50g (2oz) soft dairy toffees

25g (1oz) butter

50g (2oz) white marshmallows

50g (2oz) crispy rice cereal

25g (1oz) plain, milk or white chocolate

You will also need a loaf tin or plastic food box measuring about 17½ x 10cm (7 x 4in) and a heatproof bowl that fits snugly into a saucepan.

makes 6 bars or 18 squares

These chewy, crunchy sweets combine melted toffees, marshmallows and crispy rice cereal. You can cut them into bars or bite-sized squares.

1 Unwrap the toffees. Line the bottom of the tin or plastic box with baking parchment (see page 5). Wipe some oil over the sides of the tin or box, too.

You could make pretty bar wrappers – see page 54.

toffee crunch

This toffee crunch was drizzled with plain, milk and white chocolate.

Stir now and then.

2 Cut the butter into pieces. Put them in a small saucepan. Add the toffees. Put the pan over a very low heat until the toffees have half-melted.

3 Put the marshmallows in the pan. Keep stirring until the toffees and marshmallows have melted completely. Take the pan off the heat.

4 Add the crispy rice cereal to the pan. Stir well until everything is mixed together.

5 Spoon the mixture into the tin or box. Push it into the corners and press it flat with your fingers. Put the tin in a fridge for one hour, to harden.

6 Turn the toffee crunch out onto a board (see page 5). Peel off the parchment. Use a sharp knife to cut it into 6 bars. Cut each bar into 3 pieces, if you like.

7 Take the saucepan that fits your heatproof bowl. Fill it a quarter full with water. Put it over a medium heat. When the water bubbles, take it off the heat.

8 Break up the chocolate and put it in the heatproof bowl. Wearing oven gloves, lower the bowl into the pan. Leave for 5 minutes. Stir until the chocolate melts.

9 Use a spoon to scoop up some melted chocolate. Then, tip the spoon while moving it over each bar or square in a zig-zag shape, leaving a trail of chocolate.

Keep in an airtight container in the fridge for up to 5 days.

# vanilla kisses

 Ingredients:

2 medium eggs

1 pinch cream of tartar (optional)

100g (4oz) caster sugar

1 teaspoon vanilla extract

3 different food dyes

You will also need a piping gun or bag fitted with a medium-sized star-shaped nozzle, and 2 large baking trays.

## makes around 90

These sweets are mini vanilla-flavoured meringues with crisp outsides and chewy middles. They're dyed in pretty pastel shades.

1 Heat the oven to 110°C, 225°F or gas mark ¼. Line the trays with baking parchment (see page 5).

You don't need the yolks.

2 Crack one egg on the side of a bowl. Open the shell and let the egg slide onto a plate. Cover the yolk with an egg cup.

3 Hold the plate and egg cup over a big, clean bowl. Tip the plate, so the egg white slides into the bowl. Separate the other egg in the same way.

4 Sprinkle the cream of tartar over the egg whites. Whisk them very quickly with a whisk.

5 Keep whisking until the egg whites are really thick and foamy. They should stay in a stiff point when you lift up the whisk.

6 Add a heaped teaspoon of the sugar. Whisk it in well. Keep whisking in spoonfuls of sugar, until you have used it up. Add the vanilla and whisk it in, too.

Wash and dry the piping bag or gun and nozzle between each mixture.

7 Divide the mixture between 3 bowls. Drop several drops of one food dye into one bowl. Drop food dye into the other bowls, too. Mix the food dyes in.

8 Fill the piping gun or bag with the mixture from one of the bowls (see page 6). Hold the nozzle a little above a tray. Squeeze until a rosette forms. Stop squeezing and lift the nozzle quickly up and away.

9 Pipe more rosettes until the mixture is used up. Repeat steps 8 and 9 using the mixtures from the other two bowls.

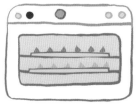

10 Bake for 40 minutes. Turn off the oven and leave them inside for 15 minutes. Then, take them out and leave them on the trays to cool.

Keep in an airtight container for up to 7 days.

You could put your vanilla kisses in a little paper bag. To make a label for it, see pages 58-59.

# stripy lollipops

## Ingredients:

18 clear boiled
sweets in several
different colours

You will also need
a baking sheet and
6 paper or wooden
lollipop sticks.

## Makes 6

These lollipops are made simply by melting boiled sweets. You can arrange the sweets any way you like to create different flavour and colour combinations.

1 Heat the oven to 130°C, 275°F or gas mark 1. Line the baking sheet (see page 5).

2 Remove the wrappers from the boiled sweets. Put 3 different coloured sweets next to each other in a row on the baking sheet.

The sweets should be touching.

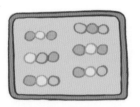

3 Arrange 5 more rows of sweets in the same way. Leave gaps between the rows, and leave room for the sticks, too.

4 Put the baking sheet in the oven for around 6-8 minutes, or until the sweets have just melted and joined together.

5 Take the baking sheet out of the oven. Be careful not to touch the sweets, as they will be very hot.

6 Straight away, push the end of a lollipop stick into the end of one row of melted sweets. Turn the stick a little as you push it in, so it is covered.

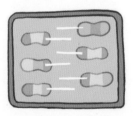

7 Push in the other lollipop sticks in the same way. Then leave the lollipops on the sheet to cool and harden.

8 Wait until the lollipops are completely cold. Then, carefully peel them off the parchment, picking them up by their sticks.

Keep in an airtight container for up to 5 days, with pieces of baking parchment between the lollipops, so they don't stick together.

# chocolate swirl slab

 Ingredients:

200g (7oz) plain chocolate

100g (4 oz) white chocolate

orange flavouring or extract

orange food dye

You will also need a loaf tin or plastic food box measuring around 17½ x 10cm (7 x 4in), a heatproof bowl that fits snugly into a saucepan and a cocktail stick.

Makes 1

This swirly chocolate slab can be flavoured with orange or mint. You could cut it into pieces and put them in homemade bags (see page 55).

1 Line the tin or box with baking parchment (see page 5).

2 Fill the saucepan a quarter full with water. Put it over a medium heat. When the water bubbles, take the pan off the heat.

3 Break up the plain chocolate and put it in the heatproof bowl. Wearing oven gloves, lower the bowl into the pan. Leave for 5 minutes. Stir until the chocolate melts.

4 Wearing oven gloves, carefully lift the bowl out of the pan. Add a few drops of orange flavouring. Mix it in well.

5 Pour the chocolate into the lined tin or box. Then, wash the heatproof bowl and dry it really well.

6 Follow steps 2 and 3 again using the white chocolate. Wearing oven gloves, carefully lift out the bowl.

Leave gaps between the orange blobs.

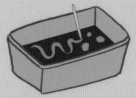

7 Add a few drops of orange flavouring and a few drops of orange food dye to the white chocolate. Mix well. Spoon blobs of this mixture on top of the melted chocolate in the tin or box.

8 Take the cocktail stick and drag the point through the blobs, making a swirling shape. Stop when all the blobs are swirled in.

Keep in an airtight container in
the fridge for up to 7 days.

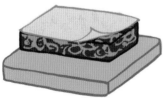

9 Put the tin in the fridge for one
hour, or until the chocolate has
set firm. Run a knife around
the edges, then turn the slab
out onto a board (see page 5).
Peel off the baking parchment.

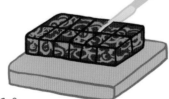

10 Leave the slab out
of the fridge for half
an hour, so it softens
slightly. Then, carefully
cut it into squares using
a sharp knife.

## other flavours

To make this recipe mint
flavoured, use peppermint
extract or flavouring and
green food dye instead of
the orange flavouring and
food dye.

# Hot chocolate straws

 **Ingredients:**

100g (4oz) plain chocolate

450ml (¾ pint) milk

2 teaspoons caster sugar

sugar sprinkles

You will also need 4 drinking straws, 4 cups, a heatproof bowl that fits snugly into a saucepan and a narrow cup, glass or mug.

**Makes 4**

These chocolate-coated straws are a fun way to make hot chocolate. You stir them in a cup of hot milk so the chocolate melts, then drink the resulting hot chocolate through the straw.

1 Put a drinking straw into each cup. Put the cups in the fridge. Then, break up the chocolate and put it in the heatproof bowl.

2 Melt the chocolate, following the instructions on page 6. Then, spoon and scrape the melted chocolate into the narrow cup, glass or mug.

Tilt the cup to make the chocolate go higher up the straw.

3 Take a straw, but leave its cup in the fridge. Dip and twist the end of the straw in the melted chocolate, so the bottom 7cm (3in) of the straw is coated.

4 Put the straw back in its cup in the fridge, with the chocolatey end down. Dip and twist the other straws too. Leave for 5 minutes, until the chocolate is just set.

5 Dip and twist each of the straws into the melted chocolate again, to make a second layer of chocolate. Put them back in their cups in the fridge for another 5 minutes.

6 Pour some sugar sprinkles onto a plate. Take one straw. Dip and twist it in the chocolate a third time. Then, hold it over the plate and scatter on some sprinkles.

7 Put the straw back in its cup in the fridge. Do the same with the other 3 straws. Leave for 15 minutes. Then, take the straws and cups out of the fridge.

8 Pour the milk into a saucepan. Add the sugar. Put the pan over a low heat. Keep stirring it with a whisk, until the milk just starts to steam.

9 Take the pan off the heat. Take the straws out of the cups. Divide the milk between the cups.

Before you drink it, make sure it's not too hot.

10 Give each person a cup and a straw, so they can dip the chocolatey end of the straw into the milk and stir it around.

Keep in an airtight container in the fridge for up to 5 days.

# mochaccino squares

 ## Ingredients:

100g (4oz) full-fat cream cheese

1 teaspoon cooking oil such as sunflower oil

450g (1lb) icing sugar, plus 2 tablespoons extra

50g (2oz) plain chocolate

40g (1½oz) butter

1 teaspoon instant coffee granules

2½ teaspoons cocoa powder

50g (2oz) white chocolate

You will also need a loaf tin or plastic food box, measuring around 17½ x 10cm (7 x 4in).

## Makes around 28

These little layered squares taste of mocha – a mixture of coffee and chocolate. If you don't like the taste of coffee, you can leave it out.

1 Take the cream cheese out of the fridge 20 minutes before you start. Grease the tin or box with the cooking oil, then line it with baking parchment (see page 5).

2 Put the cream cheese in a big bowl. Sift in 450g (1lb) of the icing sugar. Mix well. Spoon half the mixture into a medium bowl.

3 Put 20g (¾oz) of the butter in a small pan. Heat gently until the butter melts. Break up the plain chocolate. Stir it into the butter, until the chocolate melts. Take the pan off the heat.

4 Put the coffee granules in a cup and add ½ teaspoon of very hot water. Mix until all the granules have dissolved.

5 Take 1 tablespoon of the cream cheese mixture from the big bowl. Mix it into the chocolate mixture in the pan.

6 Scrape the chocolate mixture into the big bowl. Add the coffee mixture, too. Sift over the cocoa powder. Mix well. Spoon the mixture into the tin or box.

Keep in an airtight container in the fridge for up to 5 days.

7 Use the back of the spoon to push it into the corners and smooth the top. Then, put the tin or box in the fridge.

8 Put the remaining butter in a clean pan. Heat gently until the butter melts. Break up the white chocolate. Stir it into the butter, until the chocolate melts. Take the pan off the heat.

9 Take 1 tablespoon of the cream cheese mixture from the medium bowl. Mix it into the white chocolate mixture in the pan.

10 Scrape the white chocolate mixture into the medium bowl. Sift in the remaining 2 tablespoons of icing sugar. Mix well. Then, take the tin out of the fridge.

11 Spoon in the white chocolate mixture. Spread it out and smooth the top. Put it back in the fridge for 2 hours, or until firm.

12 Turn it out onto a board (see page 5). Peel off the parchment. Turn it over. Cut it into around 28 squares. Put them on a plate in the fridge for 2 hours, to harden.

To get this effect, you could sift half a teaspoon of cocoa powder over the finished squares.

Mochaccino squares

# party spoons

### Ingredients:

**For the caramel:**
100g (4oz) of caramel from a can, or a 397g (14oz) can of sweetened condensed milk

**For the chocolate ganache:**
50g (2oz) plain chocolate
50g (2oz) milk chocolate
100ml (4floz) double cream

You will also need a heatproof bowl that fits snugly into a saucepan, 10 small spoons for serving and some sweets and sugar sprinkles, for decorating.

### Makes 10

Each of these spoons gives you a delicious mouthful of caramel or soft chocolate ganache. You could make them for a party, and put out sweets and sprinkles so each guest can decorate their own spoon.

1 If you are using caramel from a can, skip to step 2. If not, follow steps 1-6 on page 50 to make the condensed milk into caramel, and cool it. Measure out 100g (4oz) of it.

2 For the chocolate ganache, melt the chocolate, following the instructions on page 6.

3 When the chocolate has melted, pour in the cream and stir it in. Wearing oven gloves, take the bowl out of the pan. Leave to cool for 20 minutes.

4 Put the bowl in the fridge for 30 minutes. Stir every now and then. The ganache will thicken. When it is like soft butter, take it out.

5 Wash your hands well. Take a teaspoon (not one of the serving spoons). Scoop up some ganache with the teaspoon. Use your finger to scrape the ganache onto a serving spoon.

6 Smooth out the ganache with your finger, so it fills the serving spoon evenly. Fill 4 more of the spoons with ganache. Scoop caramel into the other 5 spoons in the same way.

7 Put the spoons on a plate or board. Scatter over any sprinkles or sweets just before you eat them.

Chocolate beans and sugar strands

Star-shaped sprinkles

Different-sized sugar sprinkles

The caramel will keep for 1 week in an airtight container in the fridge. The ganache will keep for up to 3 days in an airtight container in the fridge.

# lime & coconut snowballs

 ## Ingredients:

1 lime
200g (7oz) white chocolate
5 tablespoons double cream
3 tablespoons unsweetened desiccated coconut

For coating:
5 tablespoons unsweetened desiccated coconut

You will also need a heatproof bowl that fits snugly into a saucepan.

## makes around 12

These round sweets combine tangy lime zest and creamy white chocolate with desiccated coconut.

1 Grate the zest from the outside of the lime, using the small holes of a grater. Cut the lime in half and squeeze the juice from one half.

Only remove the green layer – the white layer underneath tastes bitter.

2 Fill the saucepan a quarter full with water. Put it over a medium heat. When the water bubbles, take it off the heat.

3 Break the white chocolate into the heatproof bowl. Wearing oven gloves, put the bowl in the pan. Leave for 5 minutes.

4 Stir until the chocolate melts. Then, stir in the cream. Wearing oven gloves, take the bowl out of the pan. Leave to cool for 5 minutes.

5 Add the desiccated coconut and the lime zest and juice. Mix well. Put the bowl in the fridge for 1 hour. Stir every now and then.

Keep in an airtight container in the fridge for up to 3 days.

Find out on page 56 how to make a box like this for your snowballs.

You could put each snowball in a paper sweet case if you like.

6 Spread the desiccated coconut for coating on a plate. Then, scoop up a teaspoonful of the white chocolate mixture.

7 Use your hands to roll the mixture quickly into a ball. Then, put the ball on the plate and roll it around in the coconut, to coat it all over.

8 Put the ball on a clean plate. Make more snowballs in the same way. Put the plate in the fridge until you are ready to eat the snowballs.

# peppermint cream canes

## Ingredients:

a sachet of dried egg white powder, or a carton of pasteurised egg whites

5 teaspoons double cream

1 teaspoon peppermint extract or flavouring

250g (9oz) icing sugar

a little food dye

You will also need 3 paper towels and 2 chopping boards covered in baking parchment (see page 5).

## makes around 20

These soft, striped peppermint canes are made using the same recipe as the traditional homemade sweets called peppermint creams.

1 If you're using egg white powder, mix it with water following the instructions on the packaging, then put 2½ teaspoons in a medium bowl. If you're using egg whites from a carton, put 2½ teaspoons in a medium bowl.

2 Put the double cream and peppermint in the bowl with the egg whites. Mix gently.

*Keep the bowls covered while you work, so the mixture stays moist.*

3 Sift the icing sugar into a big bowl. Add the egg white mixture. Mix as well as you can. The mixture will be lumpy.

4 Use your hands to squeeze and knead the mixture into a smooth ball. Take off one third of the ball and put it in a small bowl.

5 Dampen the paper towels under a cold tap. Gently squeeze out the excess water, then spread them out. Put one over each small bowl. Put the other towel aside.

6 Make a dent in the small piece of mixture. Drop in a few drops of food dye. Fold the mixture over the dye. Keep folding and squeezing until the dye is evenly mixed through.

7 Take a piece of white mixture the size of a walnut. Roll it into a ball. Put it on one of the parchment-covered boards and roll it into a 10cm (4in) long stick. Then, cover it with the third paper towel.

8 Take a piece of dyed mixture the size of a hazelnut. Roll into a thin, 15cm (6in) stick. Remove the paper towel.

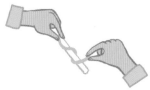

9 Gently twist the dyed stick around the white one, like this. Then, roll them again, to make one smooth stick.

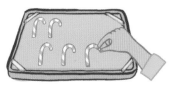

10 Gently lift the stick onto the other parchment-covered board. Bend over one end, to make a cane shape. Make more canes in the same way.

Make sure the canes don't touch.

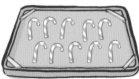

11 Cover the canes with a clean tea towel. Leave them overnight in a cool dry place (not the fridge), to dry and harden. Handle them carefully, as they will be fragile.

Pastel shades of food dye work best for these canes.

Keep in a single layer in an airtight container for up to 5 days.

## other flavours

Instead of peppermint, you could use other extracts or flavourings such as coconut, vanilla, strawberry, orange or lemon.

# Pink & white hearts

 ## Ingredients:

2 tablespoons dried cranberries

150g (6oz) white chocolate

a few drops of red or pink food dye

You will also need a chopping board, a piece of card around 5cm (2in) square, sticky tape, and a heatproof bowl that fits snugly into a pan.

## Makes around 20

These white chocolate hearts make a lovely gift. They're topped with dried cranberries, but you could use other dried fruits or nuts.

1 Cover the chopping board with baking parchment, following the instructions on page 5.

Leave gaps between the hearts.

2 Fold the card in half. Draw half a heart against the fold, like this. Cut out the heart. Unfold the heart shape. Put it on the baking parchment and draw around it.

3 Move the heart along and draw around it again. Keep doing this until you have drawn around 20 hearts. Turn the baking parchment over. Tape it to the board with sticky tape.

4 Snip the cranberries into small pieces, using kitchen scissors. Then, break the white chocolate into the heatproof bowl. Melt the chocolate, following the instructions on page 6.

These are dried cranberry pieces.

You could decorate a heart with crystallised rose petals.

5 Spoon a teaspoon of melted chocolate into the middle of a heart shape. Use the back of the spoon to spread out the chocolate, to cover the heart.

This heart was decorated with freeze-dried raspberry pieces.

Keep in an airtight container in the fridge for up to 3 days.

6 Sprinkle a few pieces of dried cranberry onto the heart. Make around 9 more hearts.

Don't add too much, or the chocolate will go hard.

7 Add a few drops of food dye to the remaining chocolate. Mix well. Make more hearts, until the chocolate is used up.

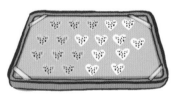

8 Put the tray in the fridge for 30 minutes, or until the chocolate is set. Then, unstick the parchment and very carefully peel off the hearts.

# coconut ice

 ## Ingredients:

1 teaspoon cooking oil, such as sunflower oil

a sachet of dried egg white powder, or a carton of pasteurised egg whites

around 480g (1lb 1oz) icing sugar

2 different food dyes

around 180g (6¼oz) unsweetened desiccated coconut

You will also need a pastry brush and a cake tin or plastic food box measuring around 16 x 16cm or 13 x 20cm (6 x 6in or 5 x 8in).

## Makes around 40 squares

Coconut ice is a moist sweet made with desiccated coconut. This recipe shows you how to make a pretty, three-layered version using different shades of food dye.

1 Brush the cooking oil all over the inside of the tin or food box. Then, line the base of the tin or box with baking parchment (see page 5).

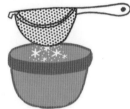

2 If you're using egg white powder, mix it with water following the instructions on the packaging, then put 3½ teaspoons in a big bowl. If you're using egg whites from a carton, put 3½ teaspoons in a big bowl.

3 Sift 160g (5½oz) of the icing sugar into the big bowl. Add a few drops of one food dye and mix until you have a smooth paste.

4 Put 60g (2oz plus 1 tablespoon) of the coconut in the bowl. Add 1 teaspoon of water. Mix well. Scrape it into the tin or box.

5 Wet a spoon. Use the back of it to spread the mixture over the bottom of the tin. Wet the spoon again. Use it to make the mixture as flat and smooth as you can.

6 Put 3½ teaspoons of egg white into another bowl. Sift in 160g (5½oz) icing sugar. Mix. Add 60g (2oz plus 1 tablespoon) of coconut and 1 teaspoon of water. Mix well.

Make this layer flat and smooth.

7 Spread the white mixture on top of the first layer of mixture in the tin or box, using the back of a wet spoon.

Make the final layer
flat and smooth, too.

Cover it with a
clean tea towel.

8 Put 3½ teaspoons of egg white into
another bowl. Repeat steps 3 and
4, using another shade of food dye.
Spread this mixture on top of the other
layers, using the back of a wet spoon.

9 Put the tin or box in a cool
place (not the fridge) and leave
it overnight, or for at least 10
hours, to become dry and firm.

10 Run a knife around the edges
of the coconut ice. Turn it out
onto a board (see page 5).
Peel off the parchment. Cut it
into around 40 squares.

This photograph shows lots of
different batches of coconut ice,
to give you ideas for different
colour combinations.

Keep in an
airtight container
for up to 10 days.

coconut
ice

# peanut butter & chocolate cups

## Ingredients:

100g (4oz) plain chocolate

150g (5oz) milk chocolate

25g (1oz) softened butter

100g (4oz) smooth peanut butter

25g (1oz) soft light brown sugar

100g (4oz) icing sugar

For decorating:

1 tablespoon salted peanuts

You will also need 48 tiny paper baking cases or sweet cases and a heatproof bowl that fits snugly into a pan.

## makes 24

These little chocolate cups have a delicious, smooth peanut butter filling. They are decorated with chopped peanuts.

1 Put 24 of the paper cases on a tray. Then, put a second case inside each one.

2 Put the peanuts in a sieve and rinse them well under a cold tap. Then, pat them dry with a clean tea towel.

3 Put the peanuts on a chopping board. Carefully, cut them into small pieces with a sharp knife. Put them aside until later.

Wear oven gloves.

There will be some chocolate left over.

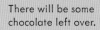

4 Break all the chocolate into the heatproof bowl. Fill the saucepan a quarter full with water. Heat gently until the water bubbles. Take the pan off the heat.

5 Carefully lower the bowl into the pan. Leave for 5 minutes. Stir until the chocolate melts. Lift the bowl out of the pan. Leave for 5 minutes to cool.

6 Spoon ¾ teaspoon of melted chocolate into a paper case. Use the back of the spoon to spread the chocolate up the sides, to the top. Do this with all the cases.

7 Put the tray in the fridge. Then, put the butter, peanut butter and light brown sugar in a bowl. Beat with a wooden spoon until smooth.

8 Sift the icing sugar into the bowl and mix well. You'll need to beat quite hard. The mixture will be crumbly.

The heat from your hands helps the mixture come together.

9 Take a heaped teaspoon of the mixture. Use your hands to squash and roll it into a ball. Make 23 more balls.

10 Take the tray out of the fridge. Put one ball into each case. Push the top of each ball gently, to flatten it.

If the chocolate is hard, put the bowl back in a pan of hot water.

11 Spoon the rest of the chocolate on top. Scatter on the chopped peanuts. Put the tray in the fridge, until the chocolate has set firm.

Peel off the paper cases before you eat these sweets.

Keep in an airtight container in the fridge for up to 4 days.

**Contains nuts**

# marzipan mice

## Ingredients:

50g (2oz) icing sugar

50g (2oz) caster sugar

100g (4oz) ground almonds

100g (4oz) sweetened condensed milk, from a can

pink food dye

For decorating:

string or ribbon for tails

flaked almonds for ears

tiny round sweets or chocolates for eyes and noses

Makes around 12

Here you'll find a recipe for a type of homemade marzipan, and instructions for shaping it into mice. If you'd prefer to shape mice from bought 'white' marzipan, just follow steps 3-8.

1 Sift the icing sugar into a big bowl. Add the caster sugar and ground almonds and stir them all together.

2 Add the condensed milk. Mix it in well, until the mixture is completely smooth. Put half the marzipan in another bowl.

3 Make a hollow in the middle of one piece of marzipan. Add a few drops of food dye. Fold the marzipan over the dye. Keep squashing and folding until the dye is mixed through.

4 Wrap each piece of marzipan in plastic food wrap. Put them in the fridge for 20 minutes. Then, cut a square of baking parchment and put it on a plate.

5 Unwrap the marzipan. Take a piece the size of a golf ball. Squeeze and roll it into a thin egg shape. Put it down on its side. Press gently, to make a flat base.

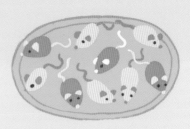

6 Cut a length of string or ribbon for a tail. Pat it gently onto the base. Take a small piece of marzipan. Pat it over the tail, like this.

7 Push in two flaked almonds for ears, like this. Add tiny sweets for eyes and a nose – or you could use the end of a cocktail stick to make little holes instead.

8 Put the mouse on the plate. Make more mice, until the marzipan is used up. Cover with a clean tea towel. Leave overnight (not in the fridge), to dry and harden.

Keep in an airtight container for up to 4 days.

To make pink ears, paint flaked almonds with pink food dye, then leave them to dry.

# creamy chocolate eggs

 Ingredients:

20g (¾ oz) softened
   unsalted butter

100g (3½ oz) icing sugar,
   plus extra for dusting

1½ tablespoons
   golden syrup

¼ teaspoon vanilla extract

orange food dye

50g (2oz) milk chocolate

You will also need 3 plastic
food boxes, a baking tray
that fits in your freezer,
a heatproof bowl that
fits snugly into a saucepan,
a big potato and 6
cocktail sticks.

Makes 6

Each of these eggs has a chocolate shell and
a creamy yolk and white inside. If you like,
you could wrap your eggs in shiny foil.

1 Line the baking tray with parchment (see page 5).

2 Put the butter in a
bowl and beat it with a
wooden spoon. Sift over
2 tablespoons of the icing
sugar. Add the golden
syrup and vanilla. Mix.

3 Sift over 2 more
tablespoons of icing sugar
and stir them in. Keep on
adding the remaining icing
sugar in the same way, until
it is all mixed in.

4 Put ¼ of the mixture into a plastic
box. Mix in a little orange dye.
Put the remaining mixture in
another plastic box. Put them
both in the freezer for 10 minutes.

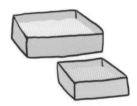

Keep in the fridge
for up to 7 days.

5 Divide the orange mixture
into 6 pieces. Dust a little
icing sugar over your hands.
Roll each piece into a ball.
Put the balls in a third
plastic box, in the freezer.

6 Divide the white mixture
into 6 pieces. Dust your
hands with icing sugar. Roll
the pieces into balls, then
flatten each ball into a circle,
around 6cm (2½ in) wide.

7 Put an orange ball in the middle of a white circle. Smooth the white mixture up and over the orange ball until it is covered. Gently roll it into an egg shape.

8 Make 5 more eggs in the same way. Put them on the lined tray. Put the tray in the freezer for 10 minutes.

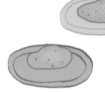

9 Melt the chocolate in the heatproof bowl (see page 6). Leave it to cool for 3 minutes. Meanwhile, cut the potato in half and put each half on a plate with the cut side down.

10 Take the tray out of the freezer. Push a cocktail stick into the big end of an egg. Dip the egg into the chocolate, coating it all over.

11 Push the other end of the cocktail stick into the potato, so the egg stands upright. Coat the rest of the eggs and stand them in the potato halves in the same way.

12 Put the plate in the fridge for 20 minutes, or until the chocolate has set. Remove the cocktail sticks. You could use the potato to make potato prints, or mashed potato.

Find out how to wrap your eggs in foil on page 54. You can use kitchen foil, or buy foil wrappers in pretty shades on the internet.

# marshmallow pops

## Ingredients:

12 regular-sized marshmallows

sugar sprinkles

around 250g (9oz) white chocolate

pink, yellow and orange food dyes

You will also need 12 lollipop sticks or wooden skewers, a heatproof bowl that fits snugly into a saucepan, and 2 glasses or jars to stand the pops in while they set.

Makes 12

These delicious marshmallow pops are made by pushing marshmallows onto lollipop sticks, then covering them in white chocolate and sugar sprinkles.

Keep in an airtight container in the fridge for up to 3 days.

These pops were made using gel food dyes. If you use liquid dyes, your pops will be paler.

1 Push each marshmallow onto the end of a lollipop stick or skewer, so the stick or skewer goes half-way through the marshmallow. Pour the sprinkles into a plate.

2 Break up one quarter of the white chocolate. Put it in the heatproof bowl. Fill the saucepan a quarter full with water.

3 Put the saucepan over a medium heat. When the water bubbles, take the pan off the heat. Wearing oven gloves, lower the bowl into the pan.

4 Leave for 5 minutes. Then stir, until the chocolate melts. Wearing oven gloves, take the bowl out of the pan.

Don't add too much dye, or the chocolate will go hard.

5 Drop a few drops of pink food dye into the bowl. Mix it in, until all the chocolate is pale pink.

6 Dip a marshmallow into the chocolate, so it's covered all over. Hold the marshmallow over the bowl. Tap the stick against the bowl rim, to get rid of excess chocolate.

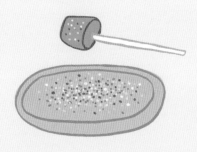

7 Hold the pop over the plate. Pick up some sprinkles with your fingers and scatter them over the chocolate. Stand the pop in a glass or jar.

8 Make 2 more pink pops in the same way. Put the jar in the fridge to set. Wash and dry the heatproof bowl.

9 Follow steps 2-8 again, but using the yellow dye. Then, do the same again, using the orange dye. Finally, do the same again without adding any dye.

They are ready to eat when the chocolate has set firm.

# lemonade candies

## Ingredients:

2 tablespoons lemonade

1 gelatine leaf

1 tablespoon golden syrup

350g (12½ oz) icing sugar, plus extra for sifting

4 different food dyes (gel food dyes work best)

4 different food flavourings

You will also need a large baking tray, a small heatproof bowl that fits snugly into a saucepan and a 2cm (¾in) plain round cutter.

## Makes around 100

These sweets are made using fizzy lemonade. You leave them overnight to turn crunchy and hard.

1 Line the baking tray with baking parchment (see page 5).

2 Put the lemonade in the small bowl. Cut the gelatine into small pieces with kitchen scissors. Add them to the lemonade, making sure they're covered. Leave for 3 minutes.

3 Fill the saucepan a quarter full with water. Put it over a medium heat. When the water bubbles take it off the heat.

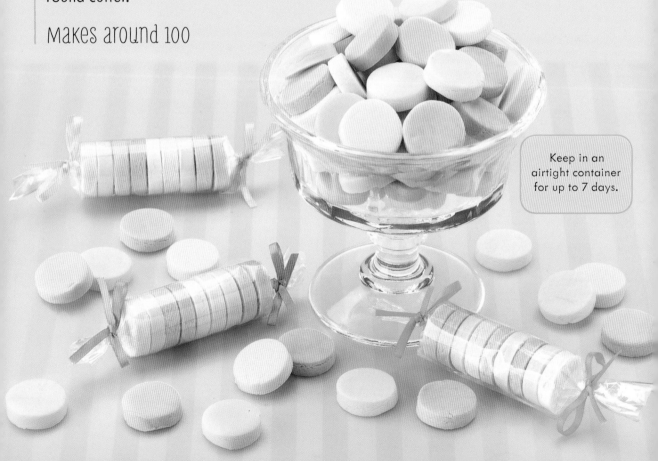

Keep in an airtight container for up to 7 days.

4 Wearing oven gloves, carefully lower the bowl into the pan. Leave for 5 minutes. Stir until the gelatine has dissolved completely.

5 Wearing oven gloves, remove the bowl from the pan. Add the golden syrup to the mixture and stir it in.

6 Sift the icing sugar into a bowl. Add the gelatine mixture. Stir until everything comes together in a ball.

7 Dust a little icing sugar over a clean surface. Put the ball on the surface. Fold, squash and squeeze it until it's smooth. Divide it into 4 pieces. Wrap 3 of them in plastic food wrap.

8 Make a dent in the fourth piece with a finger. Drop in a few drops of one food dye and a few drops of one flavouring. Sift 2 teaspoons of icing sugar over it.

9 Fold, squash and squeeze the mixture until the dye is evenly mixed through. Then, wrap the mixture in food wrap. Add dye and flavouring to the other pieces in the same way.

10 Dust a little icing sugar over a clean surface and a rolling pin. Unwrap one piece again. Roll it out until it's almost as thick as your little finger. Use the cutter to cut out lots of sweets.

11 Squeeze the scraps together, then roll them out again. Cut out more sweets. Put all the sweets on the tray. Make sweets from the other pieces in the same way.

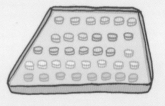

12 Cover the sweets with a clean tea towel. Leave them to dry (not in the fridge) for at least 8 hours. Then, turn the sweets over, cover and leave for 6 hours more.

If you can't get leaf gelatine, sprinkle $\frac{1}{2}$ teaspoon powdered gelatine over the lemonade in step 2.

# meringue mushrooms

 Ingredients:

2 medium eggs

100g (4oz) caster sugar

2 teaspoons cocoa powder

100g (4oz) milk chocolate

You will also need a piping bag fitted with a big, round nozzle, 2 large baking trays and a heatproof bowl that fits snugly into a pan.

## Makes around 20

These mushrooms have chocolate meringue caps and plain meringue stalks, stuck together with melted chocolate.

1 Heat the oven to 110°C, 225°F or gas mark ¼. Line the trays (see page 5).

2 Separate the eggs, following steps 2 and 3 on page 14, so the whites are in a large, clean bowl.

3 Whisk the egg whites very quickly until they're very thick and foamy. They should stand up in a stiff point when you lift up the whisk.

4 Add a heaped teaspoon of the sugar. Whisk it in well. Keep whisking in spoonfuls of sugar, until it's all mixed in.

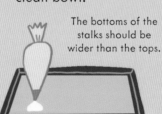

The bottoms of the stalks should be wider than the tops.

5 Spoon a quarter of the mixture into the piping bag (see page 6). Hold the nozzle just above one of the trays. Squeeze until some mixture touches the tray.

6 Keep squeezing while slowly lifting up the bag or gun, to make a stalk around 3cm (1¼ in) tall. Stop squeezing and lift the nozzle away quickly to finish. Pipe more stalks.

7 Sift the cocoa powder over the mixture in the bowl. Whisk it in. Scoop up a heaped teaspoon of the mixture. Use another spoon to push it onto the other tray.

8 Use the back of the spoon to spread the blob into a flattish, round shape. Then, make more caps in the same way, until there's one for each stalk.

9 Put both trays in the oven. Bake for 40 minutes. Turn off the oven. Leave the trays inside for 15 minutes. Then, take them out. Leave the meringues to cool completely.

Use a chopping board.

10 Use a sharp knife to cut the pointed top off each stalk. Then, melt the chocolate in the heatproof bowl, following the instructions on page 6.

Keep in an airtight container for up to 4 days.

For a speckled effect, sift half a teaspoon of cocoa powder over the caps at the end of step 8.

11 Scoop up half a teaspoon of chocolate. Spread it over the flat side of a cap, using the back of the spoon. Stick the top of a stalk into the middle of the chocolate.

12 Put the mushroom upside down on a plate. Stick the remaining caps and stalks together. The mushrooms are ready when the chocolate has set firm.

45

# toffee popcorn

## ingredients:

1 tablespoon sunflower oil

75g (3oz) popping corn

40g (1½oz) butter

25g (1oz) caster sugar

2 tablespoons soft light brown sugar

2 tablespoons golden syrup

You will also need a big saucepan with a tight-fitting lid and a big baking tray.

## makes 3-4 servings

Toffee popcorn is the perfect sweet treat to share at a party. You can put it in a big bowl or make little buckets so everyone has their own.

1 Heat the oven to 200°C, 400°F or gas mark 6.

2 Put the oil in the pan. Put the pan over a medium heat for 1 minute. Add the corn. Shake the pan gently, so the corn is in an even layer.

3 Put the lid on the pan and turn the heat down to low. After a minute or two, the corn will start to pop. Don't lift up the lid.

4 Wait for 5-6 minutes. By then most of the corn will have finished popping. Take the pan off the heat. Leave the lid on for 1 more minute.

5 Tip the popcorn onto the baking tray. Pick out any corn that hasn't popped and throw it away.

Stir with a spoon to mix everything together.

6 Put the butter, both types of sugar and the golden syrup in a clean pan. Put the pan over a low heat until the butter has melted and the sugar has dissolved. Stir.

Find out how to make little popcorn buckets like these on pages 60-61.

Keep for up to 4 days in an airtight container.

7 Pour the mixture over the popcorn. Then, use a large spoon to turn the popcorn over and over, to coat it evenly in the mixture.

8 Put the tray in the oven for 5 minutes. Then, take it out and turn all the popcorn again. Put it back in the oven for 3-4 minutes more, or until the coating is slightly darker.

9 Take the tray out of the oven and leave for 3 minutes. Turn the popcorn once more to stop it from sticking to the tray. Leave to cool completely.

# Rainbow sherbet crystals

## Ingredients:

16 tablespoons caster sugar

4 different food dyes

a few drops of lemon flavouring or extract

2 teaspoons citric acid suitable for cooking

1 teaspoon bicarbonate of soda

You will also need a medium-sized glass jar.

## Makes 1 jar

You make this sherbet by mixing sugar crystals with citric acid and bicarbonate of soda. Sherbet fizzes on your tongue as you eat it.

1 Put 4 tablespoons of the caster sugar in a small bowl. Add a few drops of food dye and a few drops of lemon flavouring. Stir until the dye is evenly mixed through.

2 Follow step 1 again, using a different food dye. Then, do it again with a third food dye, and again with a fourth food dye.

3 Spread out each of the mixtures on a plate and leave them for around 2 hours to dry. Then, crush any lumps with the back of a spoon.

Push it through the sieve with the back of a spoon.

4 Carefully put ½ teaspoon of citric acid and ¼ teaspoon of bicarbonate of soda in a bowl. Crush and mix them together with the back of a spoon.

5 Sprinkle the citric acid and bicarbonate of soda over one of the plates of dyed sugar. Mix together well. Push the mixture through a sieve onto another plate.

## citric acid

You can buy citric acid from pharmacies. Choose the type marked 'suitable for culinary use' and read the instructions on the package.

If you can't find citric acid, use the same quantity of cream of tartar instead. Your sherbet will be less fizzy.

## Dipping lollipops

You can buy lollipops to dip into your sherbet. Or make your own with the recipe on pages 16-17, but using one sweet per lollipop.

6 Follow steps 4 and 5 again, with the remaining citric acid, bicarbonate of soda and plates of dyed sugar.

7 Spoon one shade of sherbet into the bottom of the jar. Then, spoon a second shade on top.

8 Spoon in each of the remaining shades of sherbet to fill up the jar.

Keep in an airtight container for up to 2 weeks.

sherbet

You can eat sherbet by licking a lollipop or your finger and dabbing it into the crystals.

Contains optional nuts

# caramel nut fudge

## Ingredients:

100g (4oz) caramel from a can, or a 397g (14oz) can of sweetened condensed milk

75g (3oz) softened butter

400g (14oz) icing sugar, plus extra for sprinkling

100g (4oz) pecan or walnut pieces (optional)

If you're using condensed milk instead of caramel from a can, you will also need an ovenproof dish that fits inside a roasting tin, and some kitchen foil.

## Makes 25 squares

This creamy caramel fudge is studded with nuts, but you can leave them out if you prefer. You can use caramel from a can, or make your own caramel using condensed milk.

1 If you're using caramel from a can, skip to step 7. If you're using condensed milk, heat the oven to 200°C, 400°F or gas mark 6.

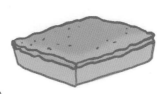 

2 Pour the condensed milk into the ovenproof dish. Cover the dish with kitchen foil, squashing the edges around the dish really well, to make a tight seal.

3 Put the dish in the roasting tin. Put the tin in the oven. Pull the oven shelf a little way out. Pour hot water into the tin, so it comes just over half-way up the sides of the dish.

4 Wearing oven gloves, very carefully push the oven shelf all the way in. Bake for 1¼ - 1½ hours, or until it has turned dark golden and become caramel.

5 Turn off the oven and leave for 30 minutes. Then, take the tin out of the oven. Carefully lift out the dish and remove the foil.

6 Beat the caramel with a wooden spoon until smooth. Leave it to cool completely.

7 Put the butter in a bowl and beat it with a wooden spoon until smooth. Add the caramel from a can, or 100g (4oz) of the caramel you have made. Beat again.

8 Sift over a little of the icing sugar and mix. Add two thirds of the remaining icing sugar and mix that in, too.

You will have some caramel left over after making this recipe. You could use it to make the party spoons on pages 24-25.

This fudge was wrapped in cellophane, then tied with ribbon.

caramel nut fudge

Keep in an airtight container in the fridge for up to 7 days.

9 Add the nuts. Sift over the rest of the icing sugar and stir everything together. It will cling together in a lump. If it's hard to stir, use your hands.

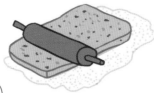

10 Sprinkle a clean surface and a rolling pin with a little icing sugar. Put the fudge on the surface. Roll it out (see page 7) until you have a rough square around 2cm (¾in) deep.

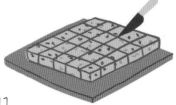

11 Cut 4 lines from top to bottom and 4 lines from side to side, so you make 25 squares. Cover with a clean tea towel. Leave to harden (not in the fridge) for at least 8 hours.

# wrappers & boxes

creamy chocolate eggs

coconut ice

vanilla kisses

# sweet wrappers

Here you can find out how to make different types of wrappers for sweets featured in this book. Some of the wrappers use cellophane, but you could use baking parchment instead.

## Bar wrappers

You will need baking parchment, patterned paper, sticky tape and ribbon or string.

1 Cut a strip of baking parchment around 12cm (5in) long and 4cm (1½ in) wide. Cut a strip of patterned paper the same size.

2 Wrap the baking parchment around the middle of your bar. Secure with tape.

3 Wrap the strip of patterned paper over the parchment. Secure with tape. You could also tie around a string or ribbon, if you like.

## Egg wrappers

For each egg, you will need a square of kitchen foil around 10 x 10cm (4 x 4in). If you want to decorate the foil with patterns, you will also need scrap paper and permanent marker pens.

Use the pens carefully, as they can stain.

1 To make patterns on a foil square, put it on the scrap paper. Draw patterns on it with the markers, going right to the edge. Leave it to dry.

2 To wrap a chocolate egg, put it in the middle of the foil. Carefully smooth the foil up and around the egg, until all the chocolate is covered.

# candy tubes

You will need cellophane, sticky tape and ribbon or string.

1 Cut a piece of cellophane around 15cm (6in) long and 10cm (4in) wide.

2 Line up some lemonade candies on it, until you have a row around 6cm (2½ in) long.

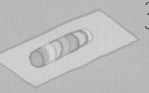

3 Bring the sides of the cellophane up and over the candies. Secure with sticky tape.

4 Scrunch the ends. Tie ribbon or string around them. Cut off any excess ends.

# cellophane bags

You will need a small, rectangular box (such as for a pack of cards), some cellophane and sticky tape.

1 Cut a piece of cellophane that's a bit more than twice as wide as your box, and a bit longer than your box.

2 Put the box on the cellophane. Wrap the sides around the box and tape them together.

3 Wrap one end around the box, like wrapping a present. Secure with tape.

4 Carefully, take the box out. Fill the bag with sweets. Fold over the top. Secure it with tape or a sticky label (see page 58).

# sweetie box

## You will need:

- a piece of tracing paper or baking parchment that's as big as the template
- a piece of card (preferably patterned) that's twice as big as the template
- an eraser
- a ballpoint pen that's run out of ink
- sticky tape

## makes 1

The template opposite will help you to make a box to hold a few of the coconut snowballs from pages 26-27. You could also use it as a gift box for other sweets from this book.

1 Put the tracing paper or baking parchment over the template. Trace over all the lines in pencil. Turn the paper or parchment over, so the pencil lines are underneath.

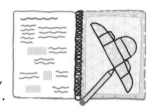

2 Put the paper or parchment over the plain side of the card so the longest dotted line is in the middle of the card. Go over the pencil lines again, pressing hard.

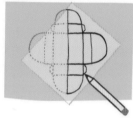

3 Rotate the paper or parchment around, then line up the long dotted line on the tracing paper with the long dotted line on the card. Go over all the lines again, pressing hard.

4 Take off the paper or parchment. The pencil lines will have come through. Cut around the solid lines.

You could secure the lid with a sticky label (see page 58) or by tying a ribbon around the box.

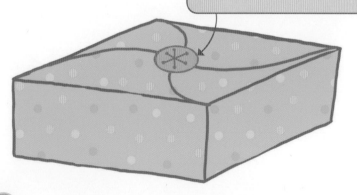

5 Put a ruler along the dashed lines. Go over them using the ballpoint pen with no ink. Rub out all the pencil lines.

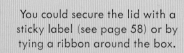

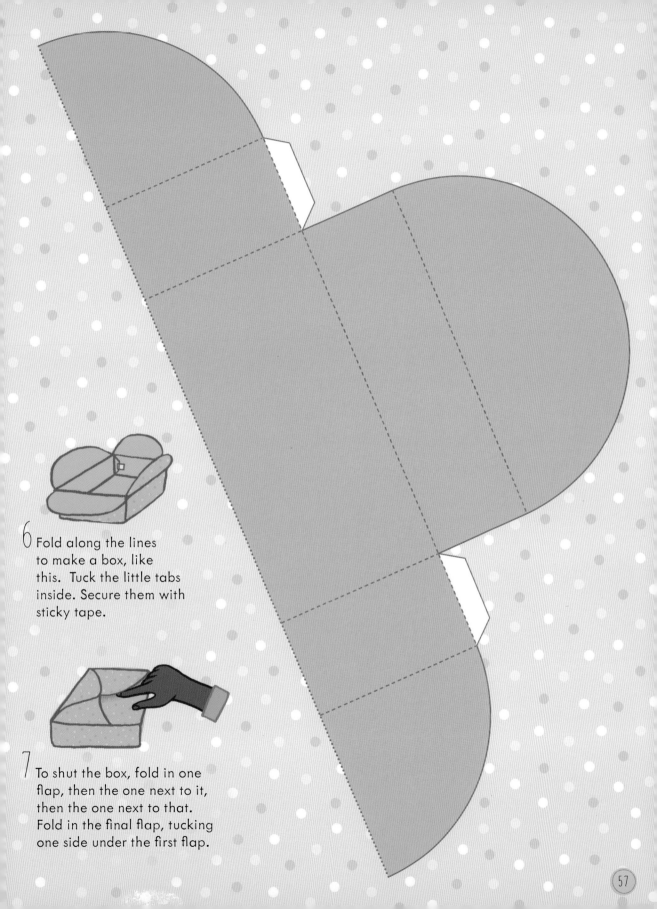

6 Fold along the lines to make a box, like this. Tuck the little tabs inside. Secure them with sticky tape.

7 To shut the box, fold in one flap, then the one next to it, then the one next to that. Fold in the final flap, tucking one side under the first flap.

# sweet labels

## You will need:

tracing paper or baking
parchment
thin card
sticky tape

You may also need a hole
punch or a cocktail stick.

## Makes 1

You can trace around the label templates on
these pages to make labels to decorate your
sweets. These labels also make great gift
tags, if you want to give your sweets as gifts.

1 Put the tracing paper or
baking parchment over
one of the templates.
Trace over the lines
using the pencil.

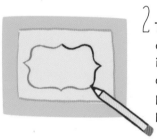

2 Turn over the paper
or parchment. Put
it over the thin
card. Go over the
pencil lines again,
pressing hard.

3 Take off the paper or
parchment. The pencil
lines will now show on
the card. Cut around
the outline, using
scissors. Then, decorate
or write on your label.

For a sticky label, cut a long
piece of sticky tape. Bend it
into a loop, with the sticky
side out. Press it onto the
back of your label.

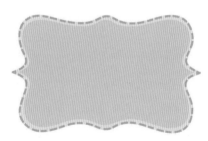

For a label to stick into a sweet, put your label face down. Lay a cocktail stick over it. Stick the cocktail stick to the label with sticky tape.

For a label to tie onto a package, punch a hole at one end of your label using one side of a hole punch.

# popcorn bucket

## You will need:

tracing paper or baking
parchment

thick paper or thin card,
preferably patterned

a pencil

scissors

an eraser

a ballpoint pen that's run
out of ink

sticky tape

## Makes 1

You could decorate your
finished bucket with a sticky
label made according to the
instructions on page 58.

Use the template opposite to make a popcorn
bucket like the ones shown on page 47. This
bucket would also make a good gift package
or party bag for other sweets from this book.

1 Put the tracing paper or baking parchment over the
template opposite. Trace over the lines in pencil.

2 Turn over the paper or
parchment. Put it on the plain
side of the thick paper or thin
card. Go over the pencil lines
again, pressing hard.

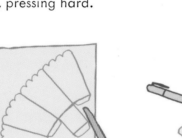

3 Take off the paper or
parchment. The pencil lines
will now show on the thick
paper or card. Cut around
the outline, using scissors.

4 Put a ruler along the
dotted lines. Go over them
using the pen that's run
out of ink. Rub out all the
pencil lines. Then, fold
along the lines.

5 Fold around the 4 long sides
of the bucket. Tuck the long
tab inside. Secure it with
sticky tape.

6 Fold in the bottom of the
bucket. Tuck the short
tabs inside. Secure them
with sticky tape.

# Index

# ingredient advice

Some recipes In this book have ingredients marked as optional. If you're cooking for someone who can't eat them, leave them out. You'll also find suggestions in ingredients lists, boxes and captions for alternative ingredients.

The list below tells you about ingredients that might be a problem for those who can't eat wheat, gluten, dairy, egg, nuts or gelatine. If you're cooking for someone who can't eat certain ingredients, check packaged ingredients, such as vanilla extract, chocolate, food dyes, bought sweets, cocoa powder or sugar sprinkles, to make sure they don't contain anything unsuitable.

### Jelly sweets
Contain gelatine.

### Toffee crunch bars
Contain dairy; bought marshmallows usually contain gelatine.

### vanilla kisses
Contain egg.

### stripy lollipops
Don't contain wheat, gluten, dairy, egg, nuts or gelatine, but check the ingredients in the boiled sweets.

### chocolate swirl slab
Contains dairy.

### Hot chocolate straws
Contain dairy.

### Mochaccino squares
Contain dairy.

### Party spoons
Contain dairy.

### Lime & coconut snowballs
Contain dairy and coconut (coconut may not be suitable for those with nut allergies).

### peppermint cream canes
Contain dairy and egg.

### pink & white hearts
Contain dairy.

### coconut ice
Contains egg and coconut (coconut may not be suitable for those with nut allergies).

### peanut butter & chocolate cups
Contain dairy and peanuts.

### Marzipan mice
Contain dairy and nuts. If using bought marzipan, check the ingredients.

### creamy chocolate eggs
Contain dairy.

### Marshmallow pops
Contain dairy; bought marshmallows usually contain gelatine.

### lemonade candies
Contain gelatine.

### Meringue mushrooms
Contain egg and dairy.

### Toffee popcorn
Contains dairy.

### Rainbow sherbet crystals
Don't contain wheat, gluten, dairy, egg, nuts or gelatine, but check the ingredients in the food dyes.

### caramel nut fudge
Contains dairy and optional nuts.

Art Director: Mary Cartwright   Senior designer: Helen Lee
Digital imaging by Nick Wakeford & John Russell

# Collins
## INTERNATIONAL
## PRIMARY
## SCIENCE

# Student's Book 2

William Collins' dream of knowledge for all began with the publication of his first book in 1819. A self-educated mill worker, he not only enriched millions of lives, but also founded a flourishing publishing house. Today, staying true to this spirit, Collins books are packed with inspiration, innovation and practical expertise. They place you at the centre of a world of possibility and give you exactly what you need to explore it.

Collins. Do more.

Published by Collins
An imprint of HarperCollins*Publishers*
The News Building
1 London Bridge Street
London
SE1 9GF

> **Browse the complete Collins catalogue at www.collins.co.uk**

10 9 8 7 6 5

ISBN: 978-0-00-758613-4

Contributing authors: Karen Morrison, Tracey Baxter, Sunetra Berry, Pat Dower, Helen Harden, Pauline Hannigan, Anita Loughrey, Emily Miller, Jonathan Miller, Anne Pilling, Pete Robinson.

British Library Cataloguing in Publication Data
A Catalogue record for this publication is available from the British Library.

Commissioned by Elizabeth Catford
Project managed by Karen Williams
Design and production by Ken Vail Graphic Design
Photo research by: Emily Hooton

**Acknowledgements**
The publishers wish to thank the following for permission to reproduce photographs.
Every effort has been made to trace copyright holders and to obtain their permission for the use of copyright materials. The publishers will gladly receive any information enabling them to rectify any error or omission at the first opportunity.
COVER: Germanskydiver / Shutterstock.com

All other photos Shutterstock.

Printed in Italy by Grafica Veneta S.p.A.

# Contents

# Topic 1 Living things in their environment

In this topic you will learn about your local environment and the plants and animals that live in different environments. You will also learn why it is important to care for our environment and find out how we can do this. Lastly you will observe and learn about the weather.

# 1.1 What is an environment?

Everything around us forms part of our **environment**. The air, the ground, the water, the buildings, the plants and the animals around us are all part of our **local** environment.

A **natural** environment is an area that has not been changed by people. Grasslands, forests, deserts, mountains and oceans are all natural environments.

A **built** environment is an area that contains buildings, roads and other things built by people. Your school and your village or town are built environments. You can find smaller natural environments in most built environments.

Plants and animals are found in both natural and built environments.

1 Name four things found in your school environment.

2 Where would you find smaller natural environments in or around your school?

3 What plants and animals are found in your local environment?

## Activities

1 Draw a picture of your local environment and label the different parts of the environment.

2 What plants and animals are found in the built environment around your school?

3 Choose one plant or animal found in your local environment. Describe it and say why you think it likes to live there.

## I have learned

- The environment is the name given to our surroundings.
- A natural environment is one that has not been changed by people.
- A built environment is one that contains buildings and other structures.

# 1.2 Comparing natural environments

**Key words**
- conditions
- hot
- cold
- dry
- wet

There are many different environments in the world, each with its own set of **conditions**. Some environments are **hot**, some are warm, and others are **cold**. Some environments have lots of water while others are very **dry**.

1 What are the conditions like in your local environment?

2 Describe how your environment changes through the year.

A

B

C

The types of plants and animals we find in an environment depends on the conditions found there. Plants and animals that like to live in hot and **wet** places are not often found naturally in cold and dry places. Plants and animals that live in water cannot survive in a dry environment.

3 Look at the environments in the photographs. What conditions would you expect to find in each environment?

4 Which of these environments are dry?

5 Which environment do you think is the coldest? Why?

## Activities

1 Look at some pictures of environments. Describe what you can see in each environment.

2 Compare two different environments. Find two similarities and two differences.

3 Choose an environment that is different to your local environment. What plants and animals would you expect to find there? Why?

## I have learned

● There are similarities and differences between local environments.

● Environments can be cold, warm or hot, and wet or dry.

● The conditions found in an environment will affect which plants and animals can live there.

# 1.3 Plants in different environments

**Key words**
- suited
- adapted

The conditions in an environment affect which plants are found there. Most plants are **suited**, or **adapted**, to their environment.

1  What plants are found in your environment? Make a class list.

Tropical environments are hot and wet. The plants that grow there have large leaves and they grow very tall.

In hot and dry environments the plants have to find ways of storing water. They usually have swollen stems or fleshy leaves. Some cacti have spines instead of leaves.

2  Compare the leaves of plants found in hot and wet environments with those of plants found in hot and dry environments. In what ways are the leaves different?

Grasslands are hot and dry for most of the year, but there is a rainy season. The grasses and other plants that live there have deep roots to help them survive when it is dry. After it rains they grow quickly and make seeds.

In cold environments it often snows in winter. Pine trees have tough needle-like leaves and springy branches that do not break if snow gathers on them. Smaller plants have tough hairy leaves that grow close to the ground. These plants can survive underneath the snow in winter.

3 Which of the plants in the photographs are found in your local environment?

4 Why do you think the other plants are not found in your environment?

## Activities

1 Choose one of the plants found in your local environment. Make a fact sheet about the plant. Your sheet should include a photo or drawing of the plant, its name, details of the conditions in which it grows, and how you think it is well suited to its environment.

2 Do your own research to find out how water plants are different to plants that grow on land. Prepare a short presentation on what you discover.

3 Design a plant that can live in a hot, wet rainforest. Draw and label your plant to show how it is suited to the environment.

## I have learned

- The conditions in an environment affect the types of plants found there.
- Plants grow in different ways to suit their environment.

## 1.4 Animals in different environments

**Key words**
- food
- water
- shelter

Animals like to live in an environment where they can find **food**, **water** and **shelter**. Some animals need special environments. For example, fish need to live in water, and earthworms need soil because they live underground.

The conditions in the environment affect which animals can live there.

The photograph below shows a river that runs through a hot, dry and rocky environment.

goat

bird

frog

lizard

These are some of the animals found in this environment.

1   How does this environment provide what each animal needs?

2   What other animals would you expect to find in this environment?

3   Why is water so important in this environment?

caracal

## Activities

1   Choose any animal that you would like to be. Draw a picture of yourself in a suitable environment.

2   Think about how you are well-suited to your environment. Make a list of at least three ways.

3   What other plants and animals are found in your environment? Make a list.

## I have learned

● The conditions in an environment affect which animals are found there.

● Animals like to live in an environment that provides food, water and shelter.

# 1.5 Suitable or unsuitable?

**Key words**
- unsuitable
- needs

Some plants and animals are found in all environments. A plant or animal can only survive if the environment provides what it needs. An **unsuitable** environment is one that does not meet the plant's or animal's **needs**.

1  Look at the pictures. Say what each plant and animal needs from its environment.

2  What features does the polar bear have that help it to survive in a snow and ice-covered environment next to a cold ocean?

polar bear

seaweed

chimpanzee

strelitzia

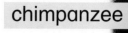

dolphin

jackal

frog

mouse

cactus

 Activities

**1** Look at the dolphin and the jackal. Which kind of environment would suit each animal? Could they survive in the same environment?

**2** Choose one of the other animals. Could it survive in your local environment? Explain why or why not.

**3** Why are you unlikely to find the three plants in the pictures growing in the same environment?

## I have learned

- A plant or animal can only survive in an environment that has what it needs.
- An environment is unsuitable if it does not meet the plant's or animal's needs.

# 1.6 Investigate a local environment

Small animals such as insects, spiders, worms and snails are found in most environments.

There are a number of small animals in this picture of an environment.

1  Count how many small animals you can find in the picture. Try to name them.

You are going to do an **investigation** to find out which small animals are found in your local environment. First you will choose an environment. Then you will **observe** it to see which animals are found there. You will **record** your observations and then compare what you found out with other groups.

Before you do your investigation, answer these questions in groups.

2 Where will you do your investigation?

3 What will you do to make sure you are safe?

4 What information will you collect?

5 Where and how will you record your information?

6 How will you tell the others what you learned?

## Activities

1 Choose a suitable environment outside the classroom. Carry out your investigation to find out which small animals are found there. Record your findings in your Workbook (pages 10–11).

2 Work with another group. Share your results. What differences are there in your results? Why do you think different groups get different results?

3 Was the environment you chose suitable or unsuitable for small animals? Give a reason for your answer.

## I have learned

- We can find information about an environment by investigating it.
- An investigation involves recording our observations and sharing our findings.

13

# 1.7 Caring for the environment

The things people do as they live and work can change the environment. We need to think about our actions and how they might affect our environment because some actions can harm or kill plants and animals.

Dirty or **polluted** water can be dangerous for most living things, including people.

1 Look at the photograph. What do you think will happen if people use this water for drinking or cooking?

2 How do you think this water became so dirty?

3 What could people do to clean and care for this environment?

## Activities

**1** Draw a picture and write a sentence to show what the word pollution means.

**2** Find examples of pollution in your local environment. Write these in order from most serious to least serious. Tell your partner how you decided on the order.

**3** Find out how water pollution affects fish and other animals that live in or near the water.

## I have learned

- Our actions can harm the environment and the living things in it.

# 1.8 What can you do?

Litter and waste are a problem in all environments. By thinking carefully about what we use, how we use it and what happens to it after we have finished with it, we can all take steps to improve our environment.

One simple thing we can all do is to follow the three Rs – **reduce**, **reuse** and **recycle**.

- Reduce means using less, for example saving water.
- Reuse means using again, for example reusing paper or plastic bags.
- Recycle means turning into something new, for example making new glass bottles from old broken glass.

The boy in the pictures is working on a project to care for his local environment.

1 What is he doing?

2 Explain how this boy's actions can help his local environment.

If we all take action to look after our local environment, we can protect it and make it better for the plants, animals and people that live there.

## Activities

**1** What can you do to improve your local environment? What materials there can be recycled?

**2** What are some of the problems caused by plastic bags? Describe what you could do to make this less of a problem?

**3** What does your school do to deal with litter and waste? What else could your school do to take care of the local environment?

## I have learned

● My actions can help to care for the environment.

● By reducing, reusing and recycling waste, we can help to improve our environment.

# 1.9 Making a difference

Water is an important **resource** in all environments.

1 Talk about how water is used at your school.

Read this newspaper article to see how one school took action to save water and care for their local environment.

2 What did the school do to save water?

3 What did the school do to get students involved in the project?

# A water wise winner

The teachers and students of Northbank Primary School won a Green Award for their efforts to save water at their school. The school saved over 150,000 litres of water last year and they now use 60 per cent less water than they did before.

## What did they do?

The school set up an action team of students to lead the project. This team carried out an investigation to find out where water was being wasted and made a plan to deal with the waste and save water. They then made posters and gave talks at assembly so that other students knew how they could help. They also sent a newsletter to parents.

Simple actions such as fixing dripping taps, collecting rainwater and using recycled waste water for the school gardens have saved thousands of litres of water. In addition, the students are now more aware of how important water is and many of them have taken steps to save water at home as well.

## Activities

**2** Describe where our fresh water comes from.

**1** Describe some ways that you could use less water.

**3** Explain why it is important to use less water.

## I have learned

- I can care for the environment by saving water.
- Small actions can make a big difference.

19

# 1.10 Weather

When we talk about the **weather** we describe the type of day it is outside. The weather may be hot, warm or cold, sunny, cloudy, rainy or dry, stormy, windy or still. These are the weather **conditions**.

1 Describe the weather in the picture.

20

**2** How can you tell it is windy?

**3** There are clouds in the sky. What does it mean when there are lots of clouds?

**4** Compare the weather in the picture with the weather outside right now.

## Activities

**1** Describe your favourite type of weather. Tell a partner why you like it.

**2** Make a list of some of the words that might be used in a weather report.

**3** Explain why it is important for us to know today what the weather might be like tomorrow or the day after.

## I have learned

- Weather is the conditions in the air around us.

- Conditions can be hot, warm or cold, sunny, cloudy, rainy or dry, stormy, windy or still.

21

# 1.11 Observing the weather

People are interested in the weather because the weather conditions affect our lives.
For example, weather affects what clothes we wear, what activities we can do and whether or not we need to water the plants in our gardens.

1 Look outside. What is the weather like today?

2 Think about how the weather affects you. Tell your group at least three ways.

Scientists **observe** and measure the weather conditions from day to day. They use special **instruments** to measure different conditions.

▲ *A wind vane shows the direction from which the wind is blowing.*

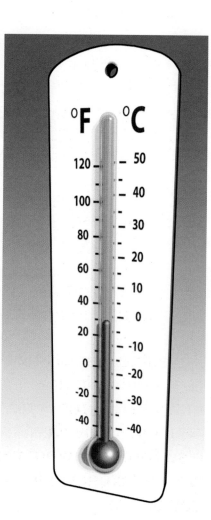

*A thermometer measures the temperature and tells us how hot or cold it is.* ▶

22

▲ *A rain gauge measures the amount of rain that falls.*

A weather **report** tells us what the weather is going to be like today in different parts of our country. Many weather reports also **forecast** what weather we can expect in the next day or two.

## Activities

1. Make a list of some of the words that people use to talk about the weather. Make sure you know the meaning of each word.

2. Draw pictures to show what the following weather words mean: stormy, windy, partly cloudy, hot, dry.

3. Some parts of the world experience cold conditions with lots of snow. Suggest how heavy snow might affect people's lives.

## I have learned

- Scientists observe and measure weather.

- They use special instruments to measure different conditions.

# 1.12 Recording the weather

You are going to observe the weather in the morning and the afternoon every day for a week. You will use a **chart** and **symbols** to record your observations.

Here is an example of a weather chart for one week. Notice that the students have recorded the weather for the weekend as well as for the school days.

| Day | Morning | Afternoon |
|---|---|---|
| Monday | rainy | cloudy |
| Tuesday | rainy | rainy |
| Wednesday | cloudy | windy |
| Thursday | sunny | windy |
| Friday | sunny | windy |
| Saturday | cloudy | windy |
| Sunday | sunny | cloudy |

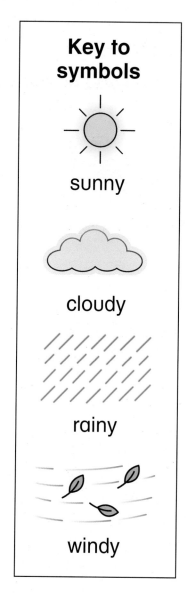

**Key to symbols**

sunny

cloudy

rainy

windy

24

1 Describe how the symbols make it easy to see what the weather was like this week.

2 On which days did the weather change from the morning to the afternoon?

3 Which day was rainy all day?

4 Which day was sunny in the morning but cloudy in the afternoon?

5 Can you see any patterns in this chart?

## Activities

**1** What symbols could you use for stormy weather, partly cloudy weather, and snowy weather? Draw these.

**2** Predict what you think the weather will be like for the next week. Make a chart to show what you predict.

**3** How accurate is the local weather forecast? Keep track of what the forecast says for the next week. Compare it with your own observations. What do your results show?

## I have learned

- A chart with symbols is a useful way of recording weather observations.

# 1.13 Play the weather game

This game is for 2–4 players.

You will need a spinner and small object to mark your place.

The winner is the first person to reach the finish line.

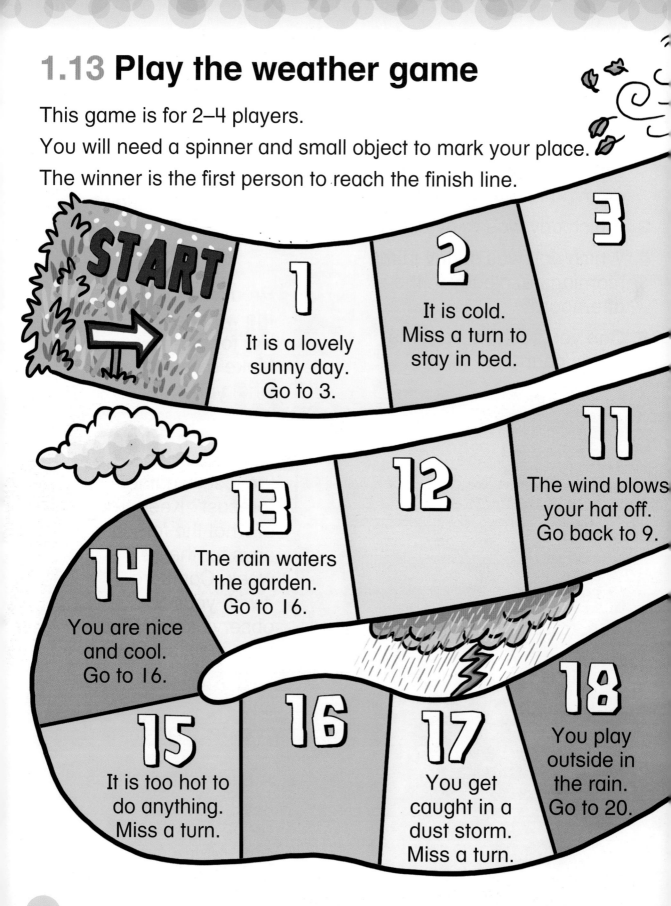

**START**

**1** It is a lovely sunny day. Go to 3.

**2** It is cold. Miss a turn to stay in bed.

**3**

**11** The wind blows your hat off. Go back to 9.

**12**

**13** The rain waters the garden. Go to 16.

**14** You are nice and cool. Go to 16.

**15** It is too hot to do anything. Miss a turn.

**16**

**17** You get caught in a dust storm. Miss a turn.

**18** You play outside in the rain. Go to 20.

**4** The wind blows you back to 3.

**5** There is a storm. Go back to the start.

**6** The weather is perfect. Go to 9.

**7** It is sunny and warm. Go to 9.

**8** It is too cold to go outside. Miss a turn.

**9**

**10** The wind dries the washing quickly. Go to 12.

**19** You catch a cold. Go back to 16.

**20**

**21** You sit in the shade to get cool. Miss a turn.

**22** You have fun flying a kite. Go to 24.

**23** There is a flood. Go back to 20.

**FINISH**

**24**

# Looking back  Topic 1

## In this topic you have learned

- There are similarities and differences between environments.
- The conditions in any environment affect the plants and animals that live there.
- It is important to care for the environment.
- Some ways of caring for the environment are keeping it clean, recycling our waste, and protecting the places where plants and animals live (their habitats).
- The conditions in the air around us are called weather.
- When we record how hot or how cold it is, how windy it is and whether it is cloudy or raining, we are recording weather data (information).

## How well do you remember?

1 Look at the pictures.

A

B

C

Write two words that describe each environment.

Explain why environment **B** is not suitable for a giraffe.

2 What might happen if people chopped down all the trees in environment **A**?

3 What kind of weather would you expect in environment **C**?

# Topic 2 Material properties

In this topic you will learn the names of some different types of rock and investigate how we use rocks. You will also learn that some materials, such as rocks, are found naturally but that other materials, such as plastics, are made by people.

# 2.1 Different types of rocks

**Key words**
• hard
• soft
• fair test

There are many different types of rocks. Some rocks are rough, some are smooth. Some are light in colour, some are dark. You can see smaller parts in some rocks.

1 Study the rocks in the photograph. Describe each one in as much detail as possible.

2 Which of these rocks are found in your environment?

sandstone

granite

slate

marble

limestone

Most rocks are **hard**, but some are softer than others.
**Soft** rocks can be scratched and they wear away easily.

Look at the rocks in the pictures again. You cannot tell how hard the rocks are just by looking at them, but you can do a **fair test** to see which rocks are hardest.

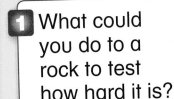

**1** What could you do to a rock to test how hard it is?

**2** You are going to test several rocks to see how hard they are. Use your Workbook (page 27) to plan your test. What should you do to try to make your test fair?

**3** What are the main reasons why your test might not be fair?

**I have learned**

- There are many different kinds of rocks.
- Sandstone, limestone, marble, granite and slate are all different types of rocks.
- I can do a fair test to compare how hard or soft rocks are.

# 2.2 Rocks are useful

**Key word**
• properties

Rocks are very useful. If you look around you will see that rocks are used in buildings, to make statues and monuments, and to make roads and pathways. They are crushed to make cement and concrete and polished to make jewellery and ornaments.

The **properties** of a rock make it suitable for different jobs.

1  Find three different types of rock used in or around your school.

2  Why do you think each type of rock was chosen for the job it is doing?

Slate is often used to tile the roofs of important buildings. Slate is hard and it splits into thin sheets. Water runs off it. ▶

▼ Granite and marble are often used to build statues or monuments. Both types of rock are attractive and can be polished to make them smooth and shiny.

▼ Sandstone blocks are used to build walls. Sandstone is easy to cut and shape but it wears away fairly easily.

Diamonds are actually very hard rocks. They are clear and shiny and they do not break or scratch easily. Diamonds and other precious stones are used to make jewellery. ▶

**3** Why do you think marble and granite are often used to make tiles or counter tops?

**4** What property of slate makes it useful for roof tiles?

## Activities

**1** You are going to make your own rock collection. Decide how many types of rock you will collect, where you will find them and how you will display them.

**2** Make a fact sheet for each rock in your collection. Include information about where you found the rock, what it looks like and, if possible, the type of rock it is.

**3** Choose three of the rocks you have collected. Suggest some possible uses for each type of rock. What properties does the rock have that make it suitable for the uses you suggested?

## I have learned

- Different types of rocks are used in different ways.
- The uses of a rock depend on its properties.

# 2.3 Natural materials

**Natural materials** come from the Earth around us, from plants or from animals.

Stone comes from rocks, wood comes from trees, cotton comes from plants. Wool, leather, feathers and horn come from animals.

cotton

stone

wood

**1** How many wooden items can you find in your classroom?

**2** Make a class list of useful materials we can get from animals.

wool

**1** Play a game to see who can think of the most ways of using plants.

**2** Which objects can be made from either stone or wood?

leather

**3** Besides stone, what other natural materials are found in rocks?

feathers

## I have learned

- Some materials occur naturally in the environment.
- Stone, wood, cotton, leather, wool, horn and feathers are all natural materials.

# 2.4 Manufactured materials

We can change natural materials to make them more useful to us. We can also use natural materials to make other materials. When we make materials we call them **manufactured** materials. Manufactured means made by people.

Concrete, plastics, glass, iron and other metals, paper and rubber are all manufactured from natural materials.

▲ *Plastics are manufactured from oil.*

1 Look around the classroom. How many manufactured materials can you find? Which one is used the most?

2 How many different kinds of metal can you name?

▲ *Paper is manufactured from wood.*

◄ *Glass is manufactured from sand.*

▲ *Concrete is manufactured from crushed limestone.*

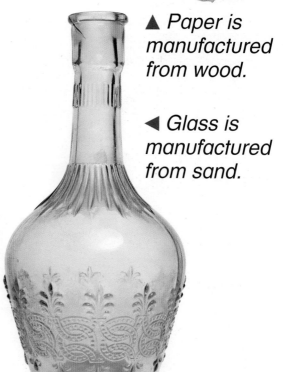

36

▲ *Iron and other metals are manufactured by melting rocks that contain the metals.*

▲ *Some rubber tyres are manufactured from oil.*

## Activities

**1** Concrete and glass are often used together in buildings. Compare the properties of these two materials and say how they are different.

**2** Paper is made from wood. How is paper different to wood? Make a list of five different uses of paper.

**3** Identify five things made from plastics. Compare the plastics and say how they are similar or different. Explain why plastic is a good material to use to make these things.

## I have learned

- Some materials are manufactured using natural materials.
- Concrete, plastics, glass, metals, paper and rubber are manufactured materials.

# Looking back  Topic 2

## In this topic you have learned

- There are different types of rocks in all environments.
- Some common rocks are sandstone, granite, marble, limestone and slate.
- Rocks can be used to build walls and roads, to make floor and roof tiles, to make statues and to make jewellery.
- Some materials are found naturally in the environment.
- Natural materials include stone, wood, cotton, wool, leather and feathers.
- People use natural materials to manufacture new materials that are useful to them.
- Some manufactured materials are concrete, plastics, glass, metals, paper and rubber.

## How well do you remember?

1 Say which type of rock you would use to make the following:
   - floor tiles
   - a monument

2 Explain why the rock you chose for the floor tiles is suitable for that use.

3 Is leather a natural or a manufactured material? Give a reason for your answer.

4 Choose the correct word:
   Glass is manufactured from **limestone** / **wood** / **sand**.

5 Choose the material that does not fit this group.

   metal    plastic    paper    wood    concrete    glass

# Topic 3 Material changes

When we use materials to make things, we often need to change the material in some way to suit our purpose. In this topic you are going to learn that you can change materials by squashing, bending, twisting or stretching them. You are also going to explore what happens to materials when you heat or cool them, or when you put them in water.

# 3.1 Materials can change shape

**Key words**
- materials
- shape
- squash
- bend
- twist
- stretch

We use **materials** to make things.
Look at all the objects in the pictures.

**1** Say what material was used to make each thing.

You can change the **shape** of some materials if you **squash**, **bend**, **twist** or **stretch** them.

**2** Which of the materials in the pictures can be squashed?

**3** Can you bend a wooden ruler?

**4** Can you twist an elastic band?

**5** What could you do to change the shape of the ball of paper?

## Activities

**1** Your teacher will give you some different materials. Work with your group to find out if you can squash, bend, twist or stretch each one. Record your findings in your Workbook (page 34).

**2** What happens to a rubber band if you twist it and then let it go? Will the same thing happen if you twist a piece of paper?

**3** Which of the materials do you think will stretch the most? What could you do to check your answer scientifically?

## I have learned

● You can change the shape of some materials by squashing, bending, twisting or stretching them.

# 3.2 Squashing materials

When we **squash** something we are actually pushing the material together or squeezing it. Think about what happens when you sit on a soft cushion. Your weight squashes the cushion and it changes shape. When you squeeze a tube to make toothpaste or cream come out, you change the shape of the tube.

**1** What is the potter doing?

**2** What is making the clay change shape?

**3** Can you squash the finished pots like this and change their shape? Why?

## Activities

**1** Make a list of things in your school or home that will change shape if you squash them. Tick the ones that will go back to their original shape when you stop squashing them.

**2** Indira has a cricket ball and a tennis ball. Predict what will happen to the shape of each ball if she stands on it to squash it. Do your own test to find out if your prediction was correct.

**3** Make a list of five materials. Write them in order from the easiest to squash to the most difficult to squash. Which is the squashiest material? What could you do to find out?

## I have learned

- When you squash something you push the material together.
- You can easily change the shape of soft materials by squashing them.

# 3.3 Does it bend?

Some materials **bend** easily. You can bend a drinking straw or a piece of card easily. We say these materials are **flexible**. The harder you push or pull these materials, the more they will bend. Too much bending can cause a material to break.

1 Find some other things in the classroom that you can bend easily. Make a list of five things that you could bend by hand.

2 Which of the materials is the hardest to bend? Why?

You cannot bend a glass plate or a brick. Materials that cannot be bent are called **rigid** materials.

3 Find three rigid materials at your school.

4 What will happen if you try to bend them?

44

Metal is a hard material, but it can be bent.

**5** Why has the nail bent?

**6** What shapes have the metal pipes been bent into?

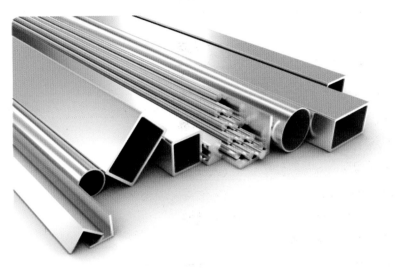

## Activities

**1** Study a paper clip. Write a set of instructions for making a paper clip from a straight piece of wire. You can add diagrams if you want to.

**2** Try to change the shape of a paper clip to make a circle of wire. How many other shapes can you make?

**3** Investigate how many times you can bend a paper clip wire before it breaks.

## I have learned

- You can change the shape of some materials by bending them.
- Flexible materials can bend. Rigid materials do not bend.

# 3.4 Twisting and stretching

When you **stretch** something, you are pulling the material apart. When you stretch it and turn it at the same time, you **twist** the material. If the material goes back to its original shape when you stop stretching or twisting it, we say the material is **elastic**.

1 What happens to a balloon as you blow air into it?

2 What makes the balloon stretch?

3 What happens if you let the air out of a balloon?

**Key words**
- stretch
- twist
- elastic

▼ *The person in this photograph is twisting the cloth to get rid of the water.*

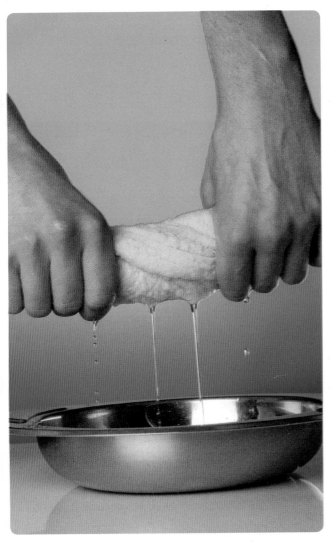

**4** Show how you would twist a piece of cloth.

## I have learned

- You can change the shape of some materials by stretching or twisting them.

## Activities

**1** Shape some modelling clay by stretching it. What shapes can you make? Draw the shapes that you make.

**2** Make a pencil shape out of the clay. Stretch your shape by pulling gently on both ends. What is the longest pencil shape you can make without breaking it? Record the results in your Workbook. (page 39)

**3** Make a fat pencil shape out of the clay. Predict how many times you will be able to twist the shape before it breaks. Test your prediction and record your results in your Workbook. What do you think will happen if you start with a fatter or a thinner shape?

# 3.5 Heating materials

When materials are **heated** they become hot.
Some materials change when they are heated.

Clay pots and bricks get hard when they are heated.

**1** Why do we need to heat clay pots and bricks before we can use them?

Bread dough gets bigger when it is left in a warm place.
When the dough is heated in an oven, it changes into bread and gets a hard crust.

**2** Describe the dough in each picture. Say what has happened to make it change.

**3** What will happen to the bread in picture **D** if the oven is too hot?

**A**

**B**

**C**

**D**

Some materials get softer or **melt** when they are heated.

**4** Name two other materials that get soft or melt when they are heated.

## Activities

**1** Investigate what happens to a slice of bread when you heat it in a toaster or over a candle flame.

**2** Compare a slice of bread with a slice of toast. How are they similar? How are they different?

**3** Does the type of bread affect how long it takes to toast? Design an experiment to answer this question.

## I have learned

- Some materials change when they are heated.
- Materials may get harder or softer when they are heated.
- Some materials melt when they are heated.

# 3.6 Cooling materials

When you **cool** materials they become colder. When you put water in the freezer it cools, gets harder and turns into **solid** ice. When you put soft margarine or butter into the fridge, or you put melting ice-cream back into the freezer, they cool down and get harder.

**1** What happens to soft margarine or butter when you put it in the fridge?

**2** Describe how you can change water into a solid block of ice.

**3** What other melted materials change back to solids when you cool them?

## Activities

**1** Your teacher will give each group a block of chocolate. Discuss how you could change the shape of this block using only heating and cooling.

**2** Carry out an investigation to change the block of chocolate into a different shape. Record your investigation on page 45 of your Workbook.

**3** Look around your classroom. Where could you place melted chocolate to make it cool most quickly? Why is this place best for cooling?

## I have learned

- Materials can be changed by cooling.
- Some melted materials can be changed back into solids by cooling them.

# 3.7 Where did it go?

Look at these pictures carefully.

**1**

I start with a glass of water.

**2**

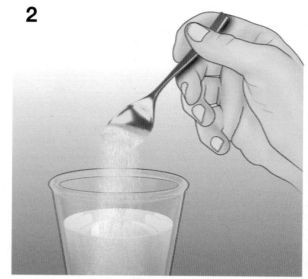

I add a teaspoon of sugar.

**3**

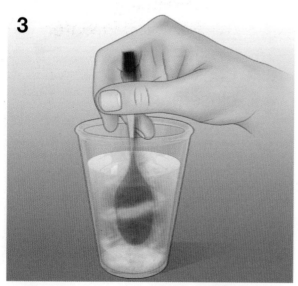

I stir the sugar and water.

**4**

The sugar seems to disappear.

**1** Where has the sugar gone?

**2** Why can you not see the sugar in the last picture?

**3** Explain how you can tell that the sugar is still in the water.

When some solids, such as sugar or salt, are added to water, they seem to disappear. We say that they **dissolve** in the water. When a material dissolves in water we are left with clear liquid and you cannot see the solid in it.

**4** Talk about why water that looks clean may not be safe for drinking.

Some solids do not dissolve in water. If you add sand to water and stir it, the sand will not dissolve. You can still see the sand grains in the water.

## Activities

**1** Predict which of these materials will dissolve in water.

| leaf tea     modelling clay |
| --- |
| bath salts     chalk powder |
| soap powder     salt |
| sawdust     jelly crystals |

Record your ideas in a table like this one:

| Dissolves in water | Does not dissolve in water |
| --- | --- |
|  |  |

**2** Create a diagram to show what happens when something dissolves in water.

**3** Make a poster to show the difference between dissolving and melting.

## I have learned

- Some materials dissolve when you mix them with water.
- You cannot see dissolved materials in the water.

# 3.8 Investigate dissolving

You are going to do a **test** to find out which materials dissolve in water.

flour

sand

sugar

coffee powder

54

Before you do your investigation, answer these questions in your group.

1 What are you trying to find out by doing this test?

2 What do you think will happen?

3 What will you need to carry out your investigation?

4 What steps will you follow in your investigation?

5 What will you keep the same?

6 What will you change?

7 How will you record your findings?

## Activities

**1** Collect the items you need and carry out your test. Record your findings in your Workbook (pages 47–48).

**2** Choose one of the materials that dissolved in water. Find out how much of the material you can dissolve in one container of water.

**3** Does the temperature of the water affect how a material dissolves? What could you do to find out?

## I have learned

- Scientists do tests to find out how different materials behave when you mix them with water.

- In a fair test we change one thing and keep all the other things the same so we can compare the results.

# Looking back  Topic 3

## In this topic you have learned

- You can change the shapes of some materials by squashing, bending, twisting or stretching them.
- Some materials change when you heat them.
- Heating materials can make them get harder or it can make them get softer and melt.
- Some materials change when you cool them.
- Cooling melted materials can make them harder. Freezing water makes it turn to solid ice.
- Some materials can dissolve in water.
- When materials dissolve in water they seem to disappear and you cannot see them in the water even though they are still there.

## How well do you remember?

**1** Describe how the shape of these materials have been changed.

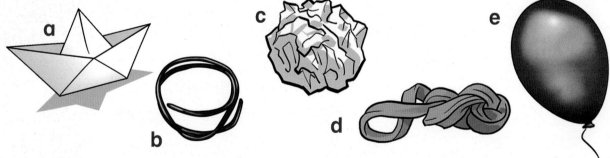

**2** What will happen to butter if you leave it in the sun?

**3** Why is it difficult to spread butter that has been in the fridge?

**4** Complete these sentences.
   **a** If you mix sugar with water it will …
   **b** You know the sugar has dissolved when …
   **c** If you mix sand with water it will …

# Topic 4 Light and dark

In this topic you are going to find out where light comes from. You will also learn more about why it gets dark and find out what causes shadows.

# 4.1 Sources of light

We need light to help us see. Objects that give out light are called **sources** of light. The Sun is a **natural** source of light and it is the main source of light on Earth during the day. **Sunlight** is very bright and strong. It is so strong that it can burn your eyes and make you blind. You should never look directly at the Sun, not even with sunglasses on.

1 Why should you never look directly at the Sun?

2 What happens to the light from the Sun when it is cloudy?

3 Can you think of any other natural sources of light?

When there is no sunlight, people have to use other human-made sources of light so that they can see.

**4** What sources of light can you see in this picture?

**5** What sources of light do you use at home?

# Activities

**1** Make a poster showing what sources of light we can use when there is no electricity available.

**2** What are the three brightest sources of light in your home at night? List them in order of brightness. How did you decide which sources of light were brightest?

**3** People cannot see well in the dark but some animals can. Find out about two animals that can see well in the dark. Make a fact sheet about one of the animals.

# I have learned

- Objects that give out light are called sources of light.

- The Sun is a natural source of light.

- Candles, flashlights, lamps and car headlights are human-made sources of light.

# 4.2 Light and dark

**Key words**
- light
- dark
- darkness

**Light** sources provide the light we need to see properly. If there is no source of light it will be **dark**. **Darkness** means there is no light.

Nicky and Zunaid are looking for a coin that dropped onto the floor and rolled under the bookcase.

**1** Why can they not see under the bookcase even though it is daytime in the classroom?

**2** Can you think of some other places that are dark during the day?

**3** What could Nicky and Zunaid do to help them see under the bookcase?

Nicky gets a flashlight and shines it under the bookcase.

**4** What is the light source in this picture?

**5** What happens to the dark area when Nicky shines the flashlight under the bookcase?

## Activities

**1** Look at different objects through a hole in a cardboard box. Record your results in your Workbook (page 52).

**2** Imagine there was no light at all for one day. Write a story describing what your day was like.

**3** Are shiny objects such as mirrors or safety vests light sources? What test could you do to find this out?

## I have learned

- We need light to see.
- When there is no light it is dark.

# 4.3 Shadows

Look at picture **A**.

Can you see the dark area in front of Joshua?

Joshua's body is blocking the path of light from the Sun. When the path of light is blocked, a dark area, called a **shadow,** forms in front of the object blocking the light.

**1** What do you notice about the shape of Joshua's shadow?

Look at Joshua's shadow in picture **B**.

**2** What has happened to his shadow?

**3** Why has the shape of the shadow changed in this picture?

**4** Here are some shadows. What do you think made each shadow?

## Activities

**1** Use a flashlight and some shapes to make different shadows. Draw the shadows that you make.

**2** Can you change the shape of the shadows? Explain how.

**3** Choose three items from your classroom. Predict and draw what their shadows will look like if you take them outside now and place them on the ground. Carry out a test to see if your prediction is correct. Use your Workbook (page 54) to record your work.

## I have learned

- A shadow is a dark area that forms when the path of light is blocked.

# 4.4 Playing with shadows

You can make fun **shadows** on the wall or a screen with your hands and a **light source**.

Work with a partner.

Make these animal shadows using your hands.

You can use a flashlight or a lamp as a light source.

Take turns to make the animals and hold the light source.

camel

elephant

bird

eagle

bear

rabbit

64

## Activities

**1** Choose a story that you like. Use cardboard to cut out the shapes of the characters in your story. Use the shapes and a flashlight to make a shadow-puppet play of your story for the class.

**2** Is it possible to make coloured shadows? Use some coloured glass objects or coloured clear plastic to find out.

**3** Bryony cut out a cardboard fish shape. She cut out the body of the fish and stuck thin tissue paper over the hole. Draw what you think the shadow would look like for this shadow-puppet.

duck

donkey

owl

goat

## I have learned

- The shape of a shadow is the same as the shape of the object that blocks the light.

# 5.1 What is a circuit?

**Key words**
- circuit
- components
- battery
- bulb

An electrical **circuit** is the path that electricity follows. Here is a simple circuit:

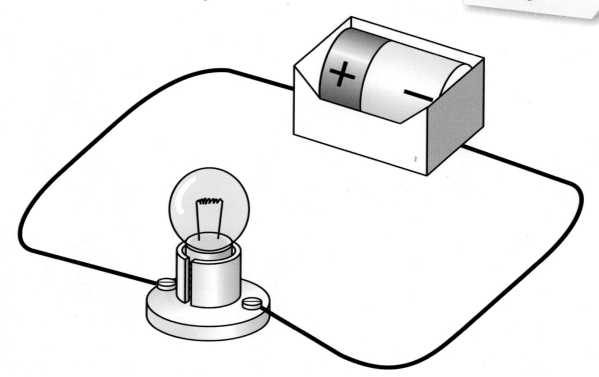

1 What do we call the part of the circuit that supplies the electricity?

2 What are the wires made of?

3 Explain why you know this circuit is working.

The parts of a circuit are called the **components** of the circuit. This circuit has three different components:

- a cell (**battery**)
- metal wire
- a **bulb**.

The bulb in this circuit will only light up if there are no breaks in the circuit. If there is a gap in the circuit or if the components are not properly connected to each other, the bulb will not light up.

## Activities

**1** Study circuits **A** and **B**. List the components used to build each circuit.

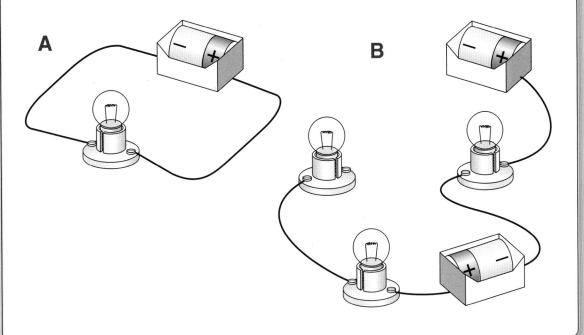

A

B

**2** Turn to page 59 of your Workbook. Predict whether the bulb(s) will light up in each circuit. If not, draw a diagram to show what needs to be added to the circuit to make the bulb(s) light up.

**3** Make a poster to teach children the difference between a complete and a broken circuit.

## I have learned

- A circuit is a path that electricity follows.
- Electricity can only move through a complete, or closed, circuit.

# 5.2 How to build a circuit

**Key words**
- components
- connect

You will need the following **components**:

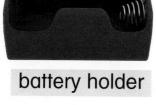
battery holder

bulb holder

wire with clamps

battery

lamp

Follow these steps to build a simple circuit using one cell and one bulb.

> ❗ Do not touch the bulb once the circuit is closed. It will get hot!

**Step 1:** Put the battery into the battery holder.

**1** How do you know which way to put the battery into the holder?

**Step 2:** Put the light bulb into the bulb holder. Screw it in carefully but do not make it too tight.

**2** Study the light bulb. What is inside it?

**Step 3:** Open the clamps and **connect** one of the wires to one end of the battery holder and one side of the bulb holder.

**3** Why does the bulb not light up at this stage?

**Step 4:** Open the clamps and connect the other wire to the other end of the battery holder and the other side of the bulb holder.

**4** How do you know if your circuit is closed?

Step 1

Step 2

Step 3

Step 4

# Activities

Amir, Layla and Jo built these circuits.

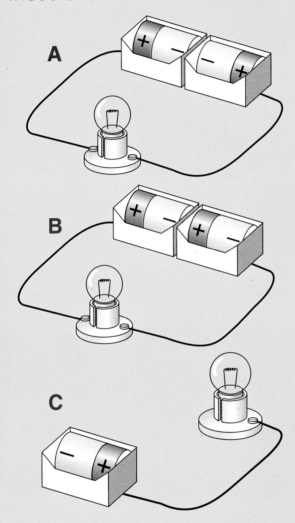

A

B

C

**1** Predict which of the bulbs will light up. Then build the circuits to see whether your predictions were correct.

**2** Try to build a circuit with two bulbs. Both bulbs should light up. Draw and label the circuit you built on page 60 of your Workbook.

**3** There is more than one way to join components to build a circuit that works. Try to build three other circuits. The bulb must light up in each one. Draw and label the circuits you build on page 60 of your Workbook.

## I have learned

- The components of the circuit must be joined properly to make a closed circuit.
- When the circuit is closed, the bulb will light up.

# 5.3 Switches

A **switch** is used to **break** or close a circuit.
We use switches to turn the electricity on or off. For
example, we switch off the lights when we go to bed at
night and we switch on the TV when we want to watch it.

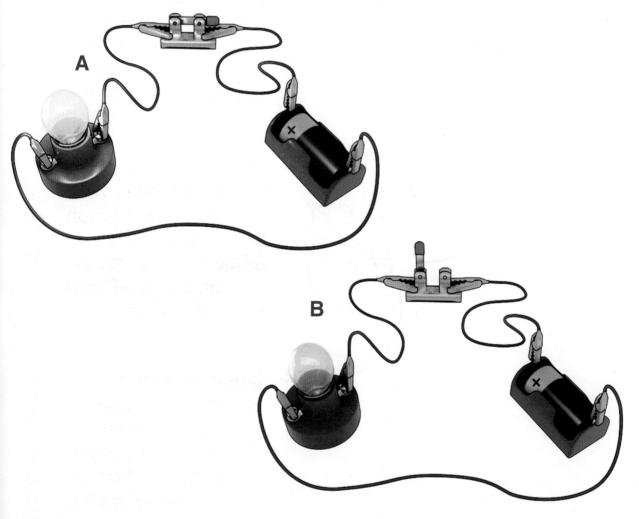

In picture **A** the switch is on and the circuit is closed.
In picture **B** the switch is off and the circuit is broken
so the bulb does not light up.

All switches work by joining and moving apart two
pieces of metal.

**1** How many switches do you use each day?

Below are some pictures of different kinds of switches.

**2** Where would you expect to find each of these kinds of switches?

**3** Why is a push switch good for a doorbell but not for the lights in your house?

## Activities

**1** Do a survey of switches found in your school. Draw three different types in your Workbook (page 63). Say where you found each type of switch and what it is used for.

**2** Which type of switch is most common in your school? Draw a graph in your Workbook (page 63) to compare the number of different kinds of switches.

**3** Many modern appliances can be switched on or off with a remote control. Try to find out how a remote control works.

## I have learned

- A switch is used to break or close an electric circuit.

# 5.4 Build your own switch

One group of students made a **switch** using a block of wood, two drawing pins and a metal paper clip. They connected the switch to their circuit like this:

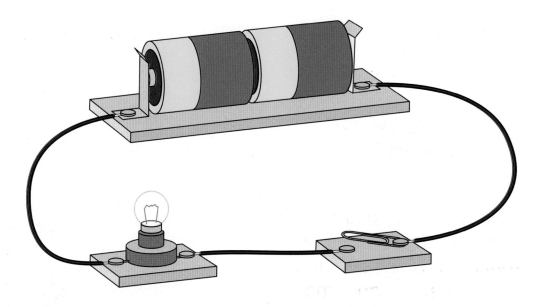

**1** Would you expect the bulb to light up in this circuit? Explain why.

**2** Describe how this switch works. ▲

Another group of students made this switch:

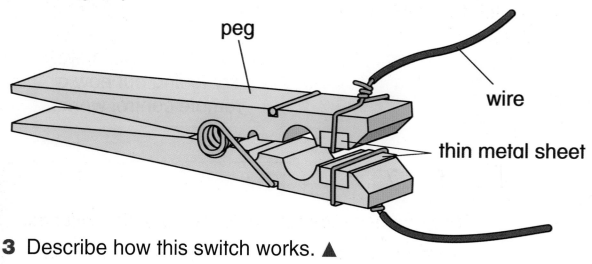

peg

wire

thin metal sheet

**3** Describe how this switch works. ▲

# Activities

**1** Compare the two switches in the pictures. Consider the materials used, how each switch works, and the advantages and disadvantages of each type. Use the table in your Workbook (page 64) to summarise the information.

**2** Can you design a better switch? Work with your group to design a different switch. Use your Workbook (page 65). Present your ideas to the rest of the class and decide which switch would work best.

**3** Amina wants to make a switch for the light at her front door. She wants to put it under her door mat, so it must be flat and thin. The switch must close the circuit if anyone stands on it so that the light goes on. Make a labelled drawing of a switch that Amina could use.

## I have learned

- You can use different materials to build switches.
- Different types of switches have different uses.

# Looking back Topic 5

## In this topic you have learned

- An electric circuit is the path that electricity follows.
- A circuit has to be complete, with no breaks, for the bulb to light up.
- The parts of a circuit are called its components.
- The battery, bulb, wire and switch are components of the circuit.
- A switch is used to open or close a circuit.

## How well do you remember?

**1** Write down three objects that work with batteries.

**2** Which of these circuits will light up?

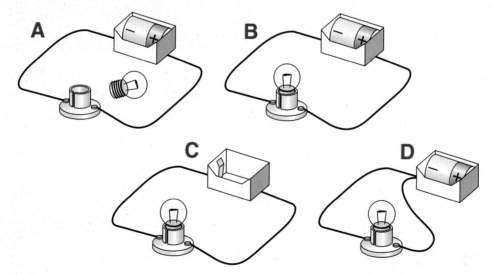

**3** Draw a closed circuit with a bulb, two batteries and a switch.

**4** Write down four things that you switch on or off every day.

**5** Describe how you would make a switch with an eraser, a metal paper clip and two push pins. Draw and label your design.

# Topic **6** The Earth and beyond

You have already seen that you can make a shadow with your body if you stand in the sunshine. You might also have noticed that your shadow is not always the same size. In this topic we are going to look at how the Sun seems to move in the sky, and how that affects the size and shape of shadows. You are also going to make a model to show why we have day and night on Earth.

# 6.1 The Earth and the Sun

**Key words**
• Earth
• Sun
• star

This is a photograph of the **Earth**. It was taken from space.

**1** Find the water and land in the picture. Explain how you can tell which parts are water.

**2** The Earth is round like a ball. Explain why you can only see one part of the Earth in the photograph.

This is a photograph of the **Sun**. Scientists take photographs like this from space using special equipment.

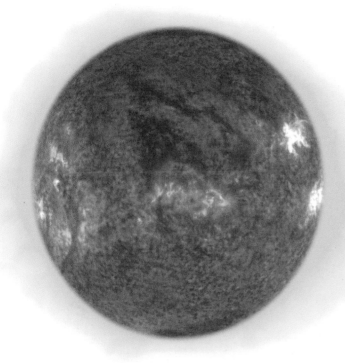

**3** Describe what the Sun looks like in this photograph.

The Sun is a **star** that gives out heat and light. The light and heat travel great distances through space to reach the Earth.

## Activities

**1** Make a poster to show why the Sun is important for all living things on Earth.

**2** Imagine the Sun did not shine for a day. Write a short story telling what the day was like.

**3** Find out about the Solar System. Make a display showing what you find out.

## I have learned

- The Sun is a star that gives out heat and light.
- The heat and light from the Sun travel great distances through space to reach the Earth.

# 6.2 Does the Sun move?

**Key words**
• sunrise
• sunset

These two pictures show the same place.

Picture **A** shows the place at **sunrise** as it is starting to get light. Picture **B** shows the place at **sunset** as it is starting to get dark.

**1** Find the Sun in each picture. What do you notice?

**2** Scientists know that the Sun does not move. Why do you think it looks like the Sun is in a different place in the sky at different times of the day?

The Earth moves around the Sun. As it moves around the Sun, it also spins like a top. It is the Earth's movements that makes it look like the Sun moves across the sky.

## Activities

**1** Work with a partner to model how the Sun appears to move even though it is the Earth that is moving.

**2** You can use a lump of clay and some straws or sticks to keep track of the Sun's position in the sky. Put the clay in a sunny place. Push one straw into the clay so that is faces the Sun and does not make a shadow. Do this every hour through the day. Look at the pattern the straws have made after one day.

**3** Copy the pattern the straws have made into your notebook. Explain why the straws have made that pattern.

## I have learned

- The Earth's movements around the Sun make it look like the Sun is moving across the sky.
- The Sun does not move.

# 6.3 Changing shadows

The shape, size and direction of **shadows** outside change during the day.

**1** What causes the girl's shadow to form?

**2** Describe how the two shadows are different.

**3** Can you explain why the two shadows are different?

Look carefully at these pictures.

**4** Describe what has changed in each picture.

**5** What effect does the position of the Sun have on shadows?

# Activities

**1** Investigate how your own shadow changes during the day. Record the information in your Workbook (page 71).

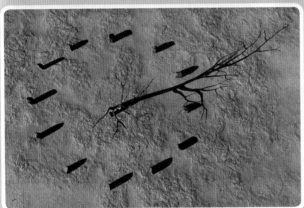

**2** A sundial is a type of clock that uses shadows to show what time of day it is. Find out how a sundial works.

**3** Design a sundial using only recycled and locally available materials. Label your design to show how it works.

## I have learned

- Shadows change size, shape and direction depending on the position of the Sun.

# 6.4 Day and night

**Key words**
• day
• night

**1** Look at these two pictures and discuss the differences between daytime and night-time.

Why do we have **day** and **night**? Read what these students think.

My dad was watching the news on TV late last night, and he said it was daytime in America while it was night-time here. How does that happen?

Maybe the Sun moves to the other side of the Earth. If that happened it would be dark here.

No, the Sun does not move. The Earth moves. Remember, we learned that?

**2** What do you think happens to cause day and night?

# Activities

**1** Complete the table on Workbook page 73 to summarise the differences between day and night.

**2** Find out the names of three countries that have night-time while it is daytime where you live. Find these places on a globe. What do you notice?

**3** Colour the map on page 74 of your Workbook to show which countries are having night-time now while it is daytime in your country.

## I have learned

- During the day we can see the Sun.
- At night we cannot see the Sun.

Even if the Earth goes around the Sun, we should still be able to see it at night. Shouldn't we? If I walk around my desk I can see the desk all the way around.

Yes, but if you spin around as you walk round your desk you will not see the desk when you are facing away from it.

# 6.5 Modelling day and night

We have day and night because the Earth spins around, almost like a spinning top, as it moves round the Sun. The Earth spins around once every 24 hours.

We have day when our country faces the Sun. We have night when the Earth spins and our country is facing away from the Sun.

As the Earth spins towards the Sun in the early morning, the Sun seems to rise slowly up in to the sky. As the Earth turns away from the Sun in the evening, the Sun seems to sink below the horizon.

**1** Read the information and look at the pictures. Discuss why we have day and night.

These students have built a **model** to show why we have day and night.

**2** What did the students use to make their model?

**3** Describe how their model works.

**4** Scientists often use models to explain science. Explain why a model is useful to show why we have day and night.

## Activities

**1** Work in small groups to make a model that will show how we have day and night. Use the information and pictures on these pages to help you. Record your model on page 76 of your Workbook.

**2** Use your model to explain to the rest of the class why we have day and night.

**3** Show where you think sunrise and sunset will occur on your model. Do you think all places in your country have sunrise at the same time in the morning? Explain your answer.

## I have learned

- Scientists use models to explain how things work.
- We can make models to show how day and night happen.

# Looking back  Topic 6

## In this topic you have learned

- The Sun is a star that gives out heat and light.
- The light from the Sun travels through space to Earth.
- The Sun appears to move across the sky but the Sun does not move.
- The Earth moves around the Sun and spins as it goes.
- The size, shape and direction of a shadow changes throughout the day.
- All places on Earth experience day and night.
- Places that are facing the Sun have daylight.
- Places that are facing away from the Sun have night-time.

## How well do you remember?

**1** Why is your shadow shortest at midday?

**2** Does the Sun really rise and set?

**3** Copy the diagram into your book and add these labels to it.

*the Sun    light from the Sun*
*the Earth    day    night*

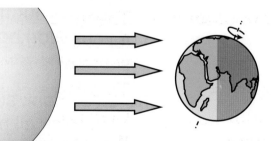

**4** Complete these sentences.

   **a** The Earth spins around once every _____ hours.

   **b** When our country faces the Sun, we have _____.

   **c** When our country faces away from the Sun, we have _____.

   **d** From Earth it looks like the _____ is moving in the sky.

   **e** We know that it is the _____ that moves and that the _____ stays still.

# Glossary

**adapted**    Something adapted has been changed to suit conditions or needs.

**battery**    A battery is a device for storing and producing electricity, for example in a flashlight or a car.

**bend**    When you bend something, you use force to make it curved or angular.

**break**    A break in a circuit is an interruption in the flow of electricity; to break something is to shatter into pieces.

**built**    The built environment is the human-made surroundings in an area or location.

**bulb**    A bulb is the glass part of an electric lamp.

**chart**    A chart is information given in the form of a table, graph or diagram.

**circuit**    An electrical circuit is a complete route around which an electric current can flow.

**cold**    Cold means having a low temperature.

**components**    Parts or elements of something. For example, a part of a machine.

**conditions**    The factors or circumstances that affect something, for example the weather. The condition of someone or something is the state it is in.

**connect**    To bring something together or in contact.

**cool**    Cool is a low temperature.

**dark**    If it is dark, there is not enough light to see properly.

**darkness**    The partial or total absence of light.

**day**    The time between sunrise and sunset.

**dissolve**    To dissolve something is to mix it into a liquid to form a solution.

**dry**    Something that is free from moisture; not wet.

**Earth**    The Earth is the planet on which we live.

**elastic**    An elastic object is able to stretch easily.

| | |
|---|---|
| **environment** | The environment is the surroundings and conditions in which something lives. |
| **fair test** | A fair test is when you change only the thing you are measuring and keep all other conditions the same. |
| **flexible** | If something is flexible you can bend it easily. |
| **food** | A food is any substance consumed by an animal or plant to provide energy. |
| **forecast** | A weather forecast is a statement saying what the weather will be like the next day or for the next few days. |
| **hard** | Something hard is firm, solid or stiff. |
| **heated** | The past tense of heat. To heat is to make something warmer, or to have warmth or the quality of being hot. |
| **hot** | Hot is having a high temperature. |
| **instruments** | Tools or measuring devices used for precision work. |
| **investigation** | The act of investigating something; an inquiry. |
| **light** | Light is brightness from the Sun, fire or lamps that enables you to see things; a lamp or other device that gives out brightness. |
| **light source** | A light source is a device or natural feature that is a source of light. |
| **local** | If something is local it relates or is restricted to a particular area; your neighbourhood is your local area or environment. |
| **manufactured** | Something is manufactured if it has been produced on a large scale, often using machinery. Human-made objects are said to be manufactured. |
| **materials** | Materials are the substances from which something is made. |
| **melt** | When something melts it changes from a solid to a liquid because it has been heated. |
| **model** | To model is to imitate or use something as an example. |

| | |
|---|---|
| **natural** | A material or something that exists or happens in nature. |
| **needs** | The needs of something are the conditions it requires to survive. |
| **night** | Night is the time between sunset and sunrise when it is dark. |
| **observe** | To observe something is to notice it. |
| **polluted** | If something is polluted, for example the air, water or soil, it is dirty or dangerous. |
| **properties** | The properties of a particular object or thing are its qualities or traits. |
| **record** | If you record information, you write it down or put it into a computer. |
| **recycle** | To recycle used products means to process them so that they can be used again. |
| **reduce** | To reduce something means to make it smaller in size or amount. |
| **report** | A report is a written or spoken account of something, for example a weather report. |
| **resource** | A substance that a plant or animal needs or values. |
| **reuse** | To reuse something is to use it again. |
| **rigid** | If something is rigid, it is stiff and does not move. |
| **shadow** | A shadow is the dark shape made when an object prevents light from reaching a surface. |
| **shape** | The shape of something is the form or pattern of its outline, for example whether it is round or square. |
| **shelter** | A shelter gives protection from bad weather or danger. |
| **soft** | If something is soft it is not hard or firm. |
| **solid** | A solid substance or object is hard or firm, and not in the form of a liquid or gas. |
| **sources** | A source is a place, person or thing from which something originates or can be obtained. |
| **squash** | To crush or squeeze something. |

| | |
|---|---|
| **star** | A star is a large ball of burning gas in space that appears as a point of light in the sky at night. |
| **stretch** | Some materials can stretch or extend to cover a greater distance than before. |
| **suited** | If something is suited to its environment it is right or appropriate. |
| **Sun** | The Sun is the star providing heat and light for the planets revolving around it in our Solar System. |
| **sunlight** | Sunlight is the light from the Sun. |
| **sunrise** | Sunrise is the time in the morning when the Sun appears. |
| **sunset** | Sunset is the time in the evening when the Sun disappears. |
| **switch** | A switch is a small on–off control for an electrical device or machine. |
| **symbol** | A symbol is a thing that represents or stands for something else. |
| **test** | To test something is to establish its quality, suitability or performance. |
| **twist** | When you twist something you turn one end of it in one direction while holding the other end or turning it in the opposite direction. |
| **unsuitable** | If something is unsuitable it is not right or appropriate. |
| **water** | Water is a clear, colourless, tasteless and odourless liquid that is necessary for all plant and animal life. |
| **weather** | Weather is the condition of the atmosphere at any particular time; the amount of rain, wind or sunshine occurring. |
| **wet** | If something is wet it is covered or saturated with water. |